Nonfiction Books by Ken Cashion:

BALL TURRET GUNNER...Weather Bad/Flak Heavy
    Soft Cover   ISBN 978-0-9985271-1-6
BERLIN GIRL...Her Story 1929 -1952
    Soft Cover   ISBN 978-0-9771187-4-8
    eBook   I SBN 978-0-9771187-8-6
LONG CAPTIONS – VOLUME ONE...Thirty-Three True Stories
    Soft Cover   ISBN 978-0-9985271-2-3
LONG CAPTIONS – VOLUME TWO...Thirty-Three True Stories
    Soft Cover   ISBN 978-0-9985271-3-0
MUSINGS FOR MUSIC LOVERS...With a Bit of History
    Soft Cover   ISBN 978-0-9771187-7-9
    eBook   ISBN 978-0-9771187-6-2
A SOCIAL HISTORY OF BRITAIN...From First Humans to the Creation of Great Britain
    Soft Cover   ISBN 978-0-9771187-2-4
    eBook   ISBN 978-0-9771187-5-5
AN AMERICAN'S TRAVEL JOURNAL OF BRITAIN: 23,000 Miles in the Left Lane
    Soft Cover   ISBN 978-0-9985271-0-9
    eBook
SOLDER SLINGER...An Engineer's Journey from the Future to the Past
    Soft Cover   ISBN 978-0-9985271-5-4
    eBook
RANDOM THOUGHTS FROM A VEERING MIND...
    Soft Cover   ISBN 978-0-9985271-4-7
    eBook
    Larger Print   ISBN 978-0-9985271-8-5
A SOCIAL HISTORY OF THE UNITED STATES FROM 1945 TO 2018...With 20/20 Hindsight
    Soft Cover   ISBN 978-0-9985271-6-1
    eBook
A RATIONALE FOR THE BASIC DIFFERENCES IN THE AMERICAN AND BRITISH SOCIAL PSYCHES
    Soft Cover   ISBN 978-0-9985271-7-8
    eBook
IT WAS AMUSING TO ME
    Soft Cover   ISBN 978-0-9985271-9-2
    eBook

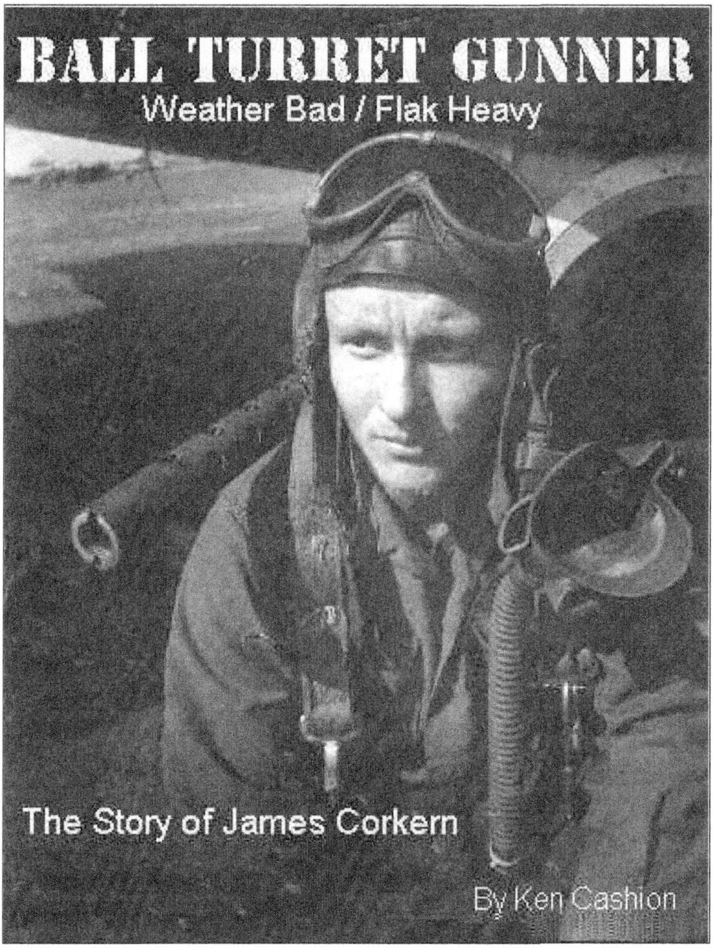

BALL TURRET GUNNER
Weather Bad / Flak Heavy

The Story of James Corkern

By Ken Cashion

Dedicated to the memory of the brave young men from the skies of yesterday.

Windmill Productions

Luddite Publishers

This is a nonfiction book and all the people and places discussed herein did exist and the events occurred as described; however, out of respect for the privacy of others, their names, the places, and dates may have been altered.

Windmill Productions
Luddite Publishers

ISBN 978-0-9985271-1-6

(Corkern photograph source)

Preface

This is not Revisionist History. This effort is not to second-guess the brave combatants in Western Europe during World War II. And these words do not address the "why" of the events. This is primarily a report, not an essay.

This is a story of a particular man and the people with whom he interfaced during a great struggle for a common good – and the story must include the aircraft that bound the people together.

These warriors were just young men who were told to do their duty, and they did it.

Most suffered.

Some suffered greatly.

Some died.

"Hero" can be defined many ways; however, the media really cannot create a hero. Dying a glorious and well-publicized death does not necessarily make a hero.

Heroes sometimes died unseen and unwept in a dirty Italian ditch.

Many died alone, tangled in the brambles of a Normandy hedgerow.

And some died slumped and shivering against cold aluminum in the unfriendly skies of Europe.

Introduction

At some time in history, the story of Man at War shifted from one of individual strength and number, to one of strategy, tactics, and machines.

In our technological age, we are sometimes more interested in the Machine than the Man, as if Man were ancillary to Machine. The more recent the war, the more likely this is; however, there was a time when separating Man and Machine was more difficult.

When the combatants of opposing sides were equally brave; when resources for waging war were similar; when the warring populations were basically the same; and when even their spiritual resources and cultural backgrounds were the same – then in those situations, the Machine became a significant consideration. It was the "tie-breaker."

When this research started, it was strictly Man-based, a man short in stature and of common background. Yet, his story is important to many people because he represents many people. As I looked at this individual more closely, my attention broadened to include the Machine; from experience, I knew this would happen.

Because I have written many essays on the subject of Man and Machines in War, I was sent a single photograph and asked to examine it to see what I could determine from it.

I did this and it turned out I was fairly accurate in my observations. Then I became inspired to learn more of the individual. As my research became more detailed, I had to take care to focus on just that individual and a particular machine...not an easy task.

There are inaccuracies in this text. I have tried to minimize their number but I have not exaggerated the circumstances reported here. Embroidering on events in history is inappropriate; reporting facts in context is exciting enough. Such inaccuracies as there may be are the natural results of integrating information from many sources into a single story.

Additionally, there may be errors which are common to researchers who become too engulfed by their subject. I apologize for these, as well as for omissions.

An effort was made to use the spelling that was current for the time.

Acknowledgments

The following pages are the result of my research and observations, as well as the combined contributions of several other people.

Harold Province, veteran of the 8th Army Air Force, 34th Bomb Group, 391st Bomb Squadron, and then Treasurer and Corresponding Secretary of the 34th Bomb Group Association provided me early information and made arrangements for me to speak with other group veterans. Harold passed away in August 2005.

In 2008, the 34th Bomb Group Association was dissolved because the number of veterans had become too few to justify ongoing activity.

Also providing information from his thorough historical database was Gary L. Ferrell, the Association Archivist. Gary lost his life in an auto accident in June 2005.

I received first-hand information from Jack Share; a special thanks goes to Jack for providing me his story and personal writings.

I was overwhelmed by the generosity of Roy Reid, the last surviving member of the B-17 aircrew which is the center of this story. Roy provided me with much of his writing and copies from his own collection. Roy is the last link of this story to the reality of what occurred those fateful months at the close of WWII.

Of course, I thank James U. Corkern, Jr., the son of my subject, James U. Corkern, Sr. It was James, Jr., who started all this by sending me the great photograph seen on the cover.

I appreciate Steve Swift and Mack McCauley of the Collings Foundation for giving me access to the Collings B-17 and particularly to the ball turret.

I thank two 34th Bomb Group ball turret gunners: Donald Forsman, who provided very interesting observations and references, and Merlin Bruning, for speaking with me about his experiences.

I gained additional insight from William Maloney, a B-24 ball turret gunner, and I thank him as well.

I always appreciate the manuscript proofing of my daughter, Julia Baker. She has years as a professional in the review of many types of government documents and technical reports.

And a continuing thanks goes to my wife, Bettie, who moves the commas and changes the singular to plural when I forget. She changes format and suggests major structural changes when she thinks it would make the story more easily read and understood. Her efforts are always appreciated.

But in spite of all this talent and knowledge, I can still introduce errors when they are not looking. These errors are mine alone.

Ken Cashion

Contents

Chapter I

The Image

In early August 2002, the author received an e-mailed image. He was asked to "see" what the image "told" him.

The image (cover) was of a young man kneeling beside a machine gun under an aircraft. That is the extent of what most people would have seen. The author saw more.

From the slope of the underside of the aircraft, he saw it was a "tail-dragger," and from a small section of a gun turret, he knew this was a B-17 Flying Fortress ball turret and he thought of the 8th AAF[1] and East Anglia, England. In the image background, well out of focus, was another B-17. That B-17 had been painted a darker color from a line at the apex of the fin down to the junction with the fuselage and then forward over the dorsal fin, but not the fuselage.

From books in his personal library, he confirmed that the darker color in this black and white image was most likely red, meaning the aircraft was assigned to the 8th AAF, 34th BGp, and it was easy enough to determine from his reference material that the 34th BGp was stationed at Mendlesham, Suffolk, England (East Anglia). The airbase was thirteen miles north of Ipswich, Suffolk.

The base was shown to be on the east side of what is now route A140 and the small village of Mendlesham is on the west side of 40. The village was less than two and one-half miles northwest of the airbase. Col. William E. Creer was the commander.

---

[1] Abbreviations – AAF - Army Air Force; BGp - Bomb Group; BSq - Bomb Squadron; Mx. - Mission; MIA - Missing in Action; KIA - Killed in Action; I.P. - Initial Point; R.P - Rallying Point.

For the date of the photograph, the author thought early 1945 because of the young man's one-piece, slip-in goggle lenses. His parachute harness (without parachute) had polished hooks where they had been rubbing against other material – the harness had been in use.

When the image was enlarged, the author was surprised to see a slight, blond moustache and a sparse quarter-inch-long goatee. If the young man was a crewman, he was liked by his pilot – and his pilot was liked by his superior; otherwise, the moustache and goatee would not have been tolerated for any period.

The principal attitude of the ball turret was with guns pointing aft, but for this well-posed photograph, the turret had been rotated with the guns forward and to the aircraft's left.

The B-17 was assumed to be a "G" model because by this date most, if not all, B-17Fs had been replaced by B-17Gs.

Almost all models of the B-17, from the Es to the Gs, could survive a phenomenal amount of abuse. It was understood by bomber crews that the Flying Fortress would bring its crewmen home when another bomber could not.

The author told James Corkern, Jr., what he thought about the image he had sent him.

James Corkern said the young man in the image was his father, James Urban Corkern, Sr., ball turret gunner on a B-17G. The other information the author provided was correct. The author began more thorough research.

—o–o–O–o–o—

Chapter II

The Man

Someone could read a few entries in James Corkern's mission log and still not know what happened. In the author's attempt to explain some of the events and put Corkern's few notes in context, there had to be more information.

"Context" is important...Context is *TIME* and *PLACE*. This is the important part of a story. Who, what, when, and where can mean little if context is not considered. Research would provide the details to establish the significance of the events – events described in a mission log with but a few hastily written words.

—o–o–O–o–o—

James Corkern graduated from Istrouma High School, Baton Rouge, Louisiana, in 1942 and then received 270 hours of electrical instruction in a trade school. He went to work for the Moss Point Barge Company in Moss Point, Mississippi.

He enlisted in the Army Air Force, September 20, 1943, and received his basic training at Shepperd Field, Wichita Falls, Texas. After basic training, he was sent to Las Vegas, Nevada, for six weeks of armorer and gunner training.

Corkern was awarded his gunner's wings and was then sent to Ardmore, Oklahoma, for crew training in a B-17. There, one year after enlisting, he was assigned to a particular B-17 combat crew.

—o–o–O–o–o—

Most gunnery teaching facilities were similar to this one at McDill Air Force Base. The photo was taken during the period of the B-17G Flying Fortress. Front center is chin turret, with student operating the remote controls for that turret. Others are ball turrets. Guns were added to ball turrets after this photo was taken.

(*USAF photograph*)

Crew photograph taken in Ardmore, Oklahoma.

From left to right, back row — Bombardier Kenneth Kessinger, Sioux Falls, South Dakota; Co-pilot Eugene Blatz, Brooklyn, New York; Navigator Roy Reid, Marietta, Oklahoma; Pilot Grant W. Kennedy, Star Lake, New York.

From left to right, front row -- Gunner Paul Thomas, LaCrosse, Wisconsin; Tail Gunner James Ballard, Wells, Nevada (or Hurricane, Utah); Ball Turret Gunner James U. Corkern, Baton Rouge, Louisiana; Assist. Engineer/Gunner Cleo Baughman, Stockton, Kansas; Engineer/Gunner Everette Riggs, St. Louis, Missouri; Radioman/Gunner Roger R. Erickson, Twin Lakes, Wisconsin. *(Corkern photograph source)*

Depending on circumstances, others occasionally flew replacement for one of these crewmen and at least one flew with other crews, but crew members generally remained together.

James Urban Corkern *(Corkern photograph* source)

After combat operational training in Oklahoma, the crew was sent to Lincoln, Nebraska, and from Lincoln, to Camp Kilmer, New Jersey. There, they would prepare for shipping overseas.

When the time came, Riggs, the engineer and top turret gunner was hospitalized and did not depart with the others but arrived later. The rest of the crew boarded the Queen Elizabeth, sharing it with 11,000 others bound for Britain.

The ship docked at Greenock, Scotland, the last week of November 1944. The crew was taken to an abandoned distillery, given a meal, and a short time later, they boarded an English troop train for the AAF replacement depot in Stone, England.

After a few days at the replacement depot, they were assigned to a bomb group, but for security reasons, just the pilot, Kennedy, knew the destination; the other crew members were told only that they would go through London.

British trains did not have open seating but had individual compartments with doors opening to the outside of the car. There were no corridors or aisles between the compartments. To change compartments, passengers waited until the train stopped at a station.

James Ballard, Cleo Baughman, "Shorty" Corkern, and Roy Reid liked to pass time playing poker, so they were together in one compartment, and the rest of the crew were in another.

The train stopped in Liverpool and the poker players, absorbed in their game, were unaware of a train change; they continued playing while their leader, Kennedy, and his group boarded another train.

After Kennedy's train left the station, an English porter came to the "poker salon" and informed the players they would have to get off. They told the porter they wouldn't because they were going to London. He said their train wasn't going to London and the one they were supposed to have been on had departed.

A nice rail agent wrote complimentary tickets for them to get on a train to London.

When Kennedy arrived in London, it was intuitively obvious that some of his crew, the crew he was to lead into battle, were lost. And one of the lost crewmen was his navigator.

This navigator, who would be expected to guide the crew through heavy overcast, weave through concentrated flak corridors, and quickly shift course from one target to the next, was lost somewhere 180 miles to the northwest.

Kennedy made arrangements with the military police that when the rest of his crew arrived, they were to be directed to their base.

After arriving in London they were first sent by military truck to Ipswich, Sussex, East Anglia, 80 miles northeast of London. From there, a base truck took them to Mendlesham; they arrived about 5 a.m.

This train trip, like all such trips, had no food service or places to buy food, so that whole day, the four crewmen had split one can of pineapple that James Ballard, the tail gunner, had slipped from the Stone, England, mess hall.

Hungry or not, the crew now had a home and an address...8th AAF, 3rd Air Division, 93rd Bomb Wing, 34th BGp, 18th BSq, Station #156, Mendlesham, Sussex, England – East Anglia.

Chapter III

The Office

The ball turret was a less-than-desirable gun station. To put this gun position in perspective, it is necessary to remember that the gunner did not take his position in the turret until after the aircraft was airborne and he was not in the turret when landing. The Sperry ball turret, when viewed from inside the fuselage, appeared as a spherical container protruding slightly from the floor.

The turret could be positioned by its own independent, electrically-driven hydraulic system or it could be positioned by internal mechanical hand cranks. It would rotate on two axes to point the machine guns: 360 degrees in azimuth and 90 degrees in elevation.

A mechanical hand crank inside the fuselage could adjust elevation to allow the gunner to enter when airborne and combat was possible.

The turret had an entrance/exit position but, when unoccupied, it was moved from that position because the machine guns would be pointing down and would strike the ground when landing. Even so, the lowest part of the turret surface was only 15 inches from the ground.

Taxiing B-17G showing ball turret location. Aircraft color scheme and markings are for a much earlier aircraft than that flown by Corkern and crew. (All Cashion photography is of Collings Foundation B-17.)

(Cashion photograph)

Attached to the ball turret and protruding inside the fuselage was an assembly between the turret and top of the fuselage. This was part of the overall rotating structure. Mounted on this upper assembly were the ball turret gunner's oxygen bottle and ammunition boxes with 400 to 500 rounds for each gun. This arrangement simplified the routing of the ammunition belts to the guns and it made the connection of hoses, tubing, cables, etc., easier.

—o-o-O-o-o—

Internal view of ball turret as seen looking forward from waist gunner's position. Door is in aft radioman's compartment bulkhead. To right is wooden ammo box for right waist gunner.

Two aluminum ammo boxes are attached to ball turret azimuth ring and rotate in azimuth with turret. Door shown on ball top is an access door for maintenance, not ball entrance.

Vertical tube secures to fuselage top and provides rigidity for turret assembly. Normally, the gunner's oxygen bottle would be mounted to the tube.

(Cashion photograph)

Internal aft view of ball as seen from radioman's door. Ammo boxes have ammo feed belts exiting boxes which would generally enter ball at two slots just under ends of feeds. Round socket between feed belts is for main power to the turret.

At far top left are right gunner's ammo feed belts.

Ball ammo boxes are secured to aluminum tube weldment attached to the main cast structure of the rotating azimuth ring.

The entire mechanism rotates in azimuth, but only the ball changes in elevation.   *(Cashion photograph)*

Normally, the ammo feed belts are suspended on springs from the short horizontal post projecting from the inside surfaces of the two ammo boxes. This would provide the clearances necessary for the feed belts to flex as ball changes elevation.

All cables and tubing had sufficient length for the extreme limits of elevation: 90°.

(Cashion photograph)

Internal view of extreme right portion of cast support of ball turret. Azimuth ring, with teeth, is secured to the aircraft floor. The cast portion of the ball has gears to engage azimuth ring teeth.

Gear box in center is for changing the ball elevation from inside fuselage. A hand crank with a square recess is placed over square shaft projecting up; this shaft intersects the elevation sector gear out of sight below. The larger lever just aft of vertical shaft engages shaft with elevation gearing. The smaller lever, forward of shaft, locks shaft in place when not engaged.

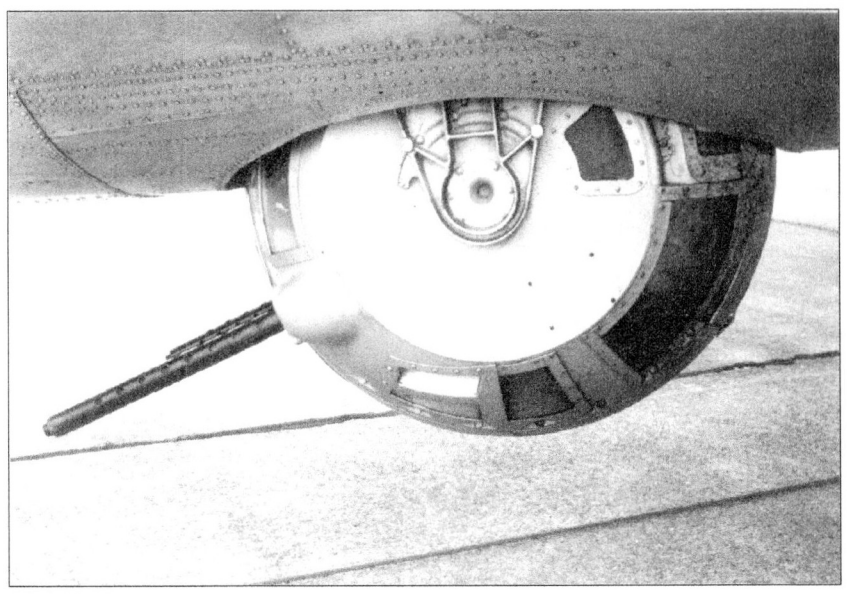

(Cashion photograph)

Ball turret with guns pointing aft. This end-of-the-war turret did not have the extent of Plexiglas glazing as earlier turrets. Near bottom of turret is the exit slot for shells and clips to fall free of aircraft. A similar slot is on other side. Trunnion extends from internal azimuth ring to ball elevation pivot. A similar trunnion is on other side.

(Cashion photograph)

Forward view of ball turret shows 13" diameter glass sighting window. This was thick, optically flat, and constituted 50% of the gunner's maximum protection against enemy gunfire and shrapnel; the hatch door provided the rest.

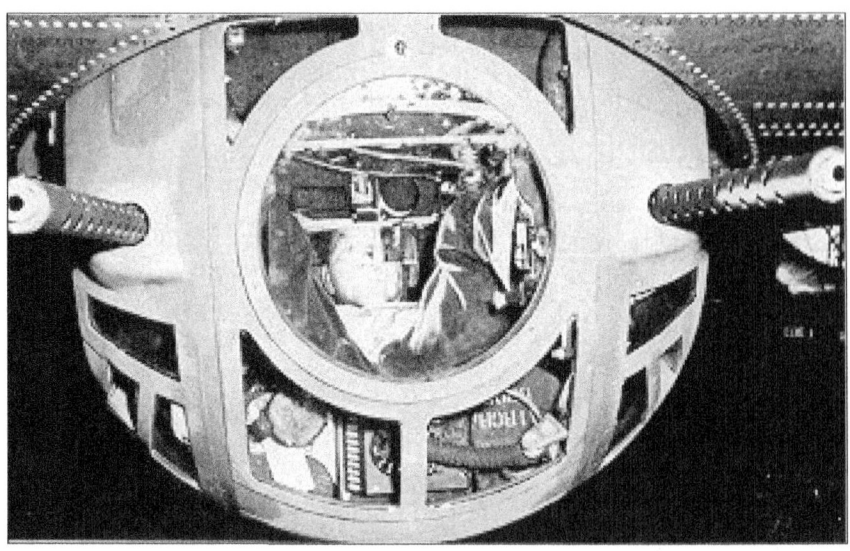

(USAF photograph)

Gunner's position in turret, sighting between his legs and out window. Seen through lower window at left is oxygen pressure regulator with output oxygen hose passing from regulator to the right over gunner's suit heater control and first aid kit seen through lower right window. Note, this turret is the common ball turret with more Plexiglas windows.

Interesting photo showing turret occupied, but hatch door open. Turret was not entered in this position, but it does show the basic size of the turret and gunner. Note unremovable door and increased glazing on sides of this common ball turret. Though a posed photograph, it appears to have been taken in a combat area.

Of interest is the elevation sector gear showing to left of ball.

(USAF photograph)

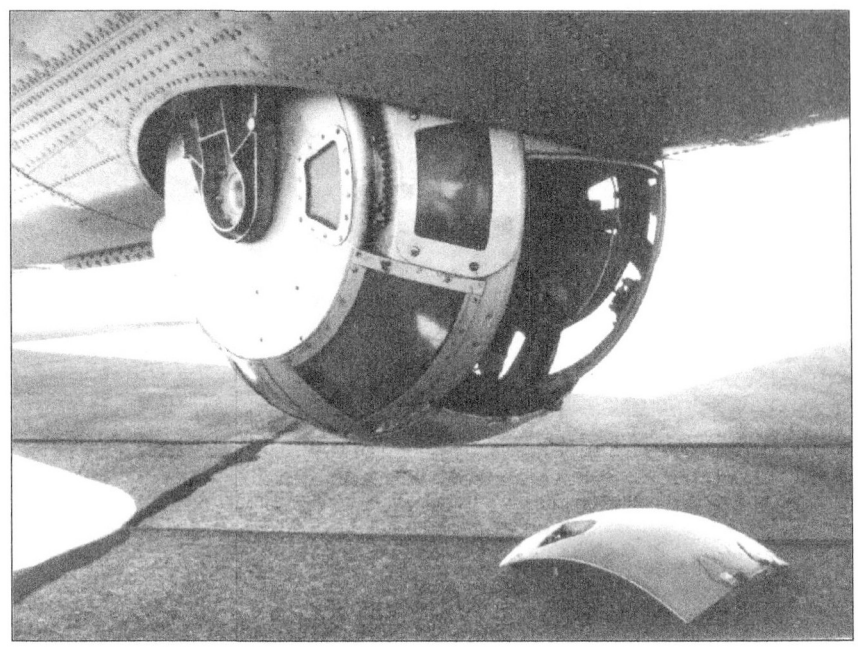

(Cashion photograph)

The last ball turret design had reduced Plexiglas glazing and a removable door as shown. Most detail inside turret is similar to the more common turret design.

(Cashion photograph)

Left interior view showing plywood seat bottom and gun mount (with replica gun). Above gun is disk-shaped manual elevation gear box.

In photo center is oxygen hose from under seat. End for gunner's mask is stowed above. Suspended in front of gunner's face is reflector gunsight. Cable in center is heel control of gunsight reticle size.

(Cashion photograph)

Upper left interior view showing hand crank at upper left for manual control for ball elevation. Panel below that is master power switch for turret.

Right top is turret control yoke with firing buttons at top of yoke grips.

Pointer knob below yoke adjusts gunsight reticle brilliance. Lower is power toggle switch for gunsight reticle.

(Cashion photograph)

Center view with computing gunsight above and heel supports below on each side of window. Small dial below right heel support is turret azimuth position indicator. To right is replica gun with two gauges below; upper is for oxygen pressure, lower is oxygen flow indicator.

(Cashion photograph)

Upper center view with hand crank for the manual elevation control to upper left.

At center is the gunner's control yoke. Tilting tops of grips changes elevation of turret (and guns); leaning the grips laterally controls turret azimuth position. Gun firing buttons are on top of grips. White wires coming from bottom of each control grip are the electrical connections to fire guns. The major assembly to which the yoke is attached is the principal hydraulic unit. On back side (out of view) is large electric motor for driving hydraulic pump. Movement of ball is controlled through valves driving hydraulic motors.

(Cashion photograph)

Upper right view. To right of gunsight is lever to engage hand crank for manual azimuth control. Hand crank is out of view, but lower portion is seen with shaft aligned with gears above chain.

Below left is right heel support with toe-operated intercom switch.

Top of oxygen pressure gauge is just visible at lower right corner.

(Cashion photograph)

Guns pointing aft in stowed position. Note square camera port just aft of turret.

The whole turret assembly weighed 1,050 pounds.

The turret was normally positioned with the guns near the undersurface of the aircraft and pointing aft. This protected the glass sighting window and guns from ground debris when taxiing and from the usual oil leaks in the aircraft's four radial engines.

When airborne, to enter the turret, a hand crank was placed on the square end of a shaft protruding from a small gear box on the right side of the azimuth ring. The crank would be rotated to lower the guns from horizontal to near straight down. This would also position the turret's hatch to the entrance/exit position facing up inside the fuselage.

The two hatch door latches would be released and the door opened. The gunner would step through this hatch, position his heels on two supports, and then lower himself to sit on a small plywood seat. The door would be closed and he would reach over his shoulders to rotate the latches to the locked position.

The door thickness would protect him against some shrapnel, .30 caliber bullets or smaller. This, and the thick window between the guns, was his only protection. (German fighter planes had both machine guns and cannons; all larger than .30 caliber.)

Inside, the gunner sat in a fetal position but with his legs apart and his knees nearly the elevation of his shoulders when guns were in the horizontal position. There were small crescents protruding on each side of the main window and these held his heels in place.

He actually sighted the attacking fighters between his legs and out the 13" diameter, optically flat window. The other smaller windows were curved Plexiglas and had distortion.

In one position, he could look straight down, in another he might be near horizontal.

Gun stations were to be manned anytime there was a possibility of fighter attack, and since bombers had been shot down over their own bases, this meant that some gunners were at their stations from very early to very late in the missions. This often resulted in a ball turret gunner being in his cramped and awkward position for 7 hours and sometimes as much as 9 hours.

To each side of the gunner's head was the breech of a .50 caliber machine gun. When firing, the shells would exit from each breech at 750 rounds a minute toward the interior of the turret. They would collect momentarily in a hopper and then slide down two chutes to fall free of the turret and aircraft.

The gunner would have been wearing a heated suit plus other apparel and on top of all that, his parachute harness. The parachute clipped to that harness.

The suit was heated electrically and there was an electrical outlet with a manual temperature control just under the forward center of his seat. A bulky, heated suit would take up room; a smaller one would have close contact to the body anywhere the suit was being pulled tight, such as at the knees, elbows, or crotch. These would get too hot while other parts of the body would be uncomfortably cold.

In spite of this, it was sometimes so cold at altitude that the interior turret surface would cover with frost, and frostbite was not uncommon. This was not a wholesome environment, yet the gunners spent a lot of time in it.

The gunner had yokes, levers, and switches to operate. There was a K-4 computing gunsight hanging in front of his face, interior lighting control, and the gun turret controls. Two D-ring handles near his ankles could be pulled so that by simple pulleys and cables, the guns could be charged.

To his lower right was a high-pressure oxygen gauge, and still lower, an oxygen flow indicator. Just under the forward right edge of his seat was the oxygen regulator. The high pressure entered the right side and the adjusted, lower pressure exited on the left side. That side had the oxygen hose that connected to his oxygen mask. The gunner could reach just under that seat edge and move a lever right or left. If he moved it left, he received a normal mixture of oxygen, if he moved it right, he received 100% oxygen.

Under the forward left edge of the seat was his first-aid kit.

Just above the right heel support was a toe-operated, push-to-talk intercom button.

The left heel support had a spring-loaded mechanism by which the gunner could push with his heel and change the size of the gunsight's aiming reticle. Adjusting this illuminated ring to the size of the attacking fighter provided a range finder input to the computing gunsight so the distance from bomber to target (the range) would be set in the computer.

With the range-to-target established, the computing gunsight required an input for the true airspeed of the bomber. The gunner received this information from the pilot and set it into the computer by knobs on the left side of the gunsight; this was not changed often.

While the gunner was changing the position of the turret to keep the attacking fighter in his gunsight, the changes in the turret's azimuth and elevation were being input automatically to the computing gunsight. Then the computer made the calculations and adjusted the gunsight so that if the gunner had the fighter in his gunsight, the guns would be "leading" the fighter by the proper amount and direction. This removed much guesswork for the gunner and increased the accuracy.

Two grips on a yoke near the gunsight controlled the hydraulic valves which moved the turret, thereby aiming the guns. At the end of each handle was a firing button that would fire both guns. An automatic firing interrupter prevented the guns from shooting the lower arcs of the bomber's props.

Tilting the yoke backward and forward changed the turret's elevation; leaning the yoke left and right changed the azimuth. The distance the yoke was moved determined how fast the turret moved.

The target would first appear as a small "x" with a gray exhaust plume. The gunners generally had to rely on the intercom to notify each other when they might have a target. The ball turret gunner had a good view below the aircraft and the top turret gunner a good view above. It was difficult for a fighter to make a surprise attack on a formation.

Flying at 20,000 feet-plus, in enemy territory, the ball turret gunner had a lot of sky to defend.

Crewmen shared many hazards, but the ball turret gunner had a unique one. If a B-17 landed with the landing gear retracted (and this was not uncommon) the ball turret would be crushed and grated into small pieces as the heavy bomber slid along the ground with its full weight on the turret. The ball turret was the lowest part of the aircraft with landing gear up – or collapsed.

The B-24 Liberator had a similar turret, but it retracted into the fuselage. This was necessary because the B-24's tricycle landing gear and high wing placed the fuselage too close to the ground for an exposed turret.

In the case of a B-17 gear-up landing, if there was sufficient time and the crew was able, the entire ball turret assembly could be released from the aircraft. This required two crewmen to work quickly removing four bolts and then hammering a locking bolt free. Landing with gear up and the turret in position caused unnecessary damage to the fuselage, but turrets were not often dropped.

Prior to a normal landing, the turret would be rotated to the exit position (machine guns pointing down), the hatch door unlatched and opened, and then the gunner could rise up to step back onto the aircraft floor and relative safety with other crewmen. The door would be closed and latched from outside and then it would be elevated by hand crank to rotate the machine guns to the landing position.

German fighter planes, as well as anti-aircraft ground fire, used explosive shells. The fighters also had standard, rapid-fire machine guns. It was altogether possible that a hit near the turret could tear or distort metal so that the turret could not rotate to the exit position. Even with the landing gear down, if there had been other battle damage, there was no way of knowing if the landing gear would stay down when the aircraft experienced landing loads; they did collapse on occasion, crushing the ball turret.

The turret gunner could easily leave the turret when the door was outside the aircraft. But he would be without his parachute. It would be in the aircraft; there was not enough room for the gunner and his parachute in the turret.

On all missions, after the aircraft had reached the desired altitude and was on its way to the target, each gunner tested the operation of his position as thoroughly as possible.

The crew navigator, Roy Reid, related the following account to the author and it gives a little better perspective on this ball turret gun station, as well as the resourcefulness of the crew.

On one mission (mission number no longer remembered), "Shorty" Corkern had entered the turret and fastened his safety straps. When he closed the small door, he apparently failed to completely secure the latches.

After he had rotated the turret to elevate the guns, the improperly latched door came loose.

This was a shock when the back of his seat popped away from him and he was hit with the cold and noise of 180-mph wind.

With the door unlatched, he could not rotate the turret to the exit position. The open door could damage the turret and possibly lock him in the turret until the aircraft could land.

There was no "Plan B" for these circumstances.

The crewmen received a very "serious and scary" call from "Shorty" telling them what had happened. "Shorty" could do nothing to remedy the situation.

No one knew how to get "Shorty" back in the fuselage.

The pilot, Kennedy, quickly got permission to remove their aircraft from the formation. (But he was to stay in contact.)

This was a bad situation. They were within range of German fighters with no protection from the formation.

And they were without a ball turret gunner.

They were flying at 10,000 feet and "Shorty" was in the lowest part of the aircraft, virtually outside the aircraft, with only straps holding him in. He could not do anything but talk to his crewmates – and stare at the ground two miles below.

Then the assistant flight engineer, Cleo Baughman, had an idea.

In the floor just aft of the ball turret was a covered camera port. They removed the covering from this port and Corkern rotated the turret in azimuth until the hatch was facing the tail and the camera port.

Baughman removed his right boot and started lowering his leg through the 8-inch square camera port. The camera port is 15 inches from the turret door. Baughman managed to reach the turret hatch with his foot and push the hatch door in place, but still it could not be latched.

Baughman kept pressure on the door as "Shorty" started to slowly alter the turret elevation until the edge of the door reached the skin of the fuselage and finally cleared the small space between the ball and the geared azimuth ring in the aircraft floor. The door was secured properly and the aircraft rejoined the formation for the mission.

Reid said, "This was a great relief to all of the crew."

Reid closed his story, "Shorty made sure that didn't happen again."

—o-o-O-o-o—

William Maloney, ball turret gunner on a B-24, had a door come open and break free. He had to physically hold himself in while getting the turret back in the proper position to have it raised back into the aircraft. The B-24 turret had to be in the correct position both in elevation and azimuth before it could be retracted into the exit position.

The ball turret gunners the author spoke with seemed to have a common theme; they were not particularly afraid they would fall out; however, they were all concerned that they would be trapped inside.

One ball turret gunner did not use his straps because he was afraid the latching mechanism might not release. Another ball turret gunner started using his straps only after he did almost fall out.

These stories are examples of the hazards the ball turret gunners faced, and it was unusual when someone could help them.

The ball turret was a cramped and solitary gun station.

—o–o–O–o–o—

Chapter IV

The Missions Begin

The 34th BGp had been flying B-24 Liberators since the group's first mission on May 23, 1944. In early September 1944, they changed over to B-17s and flew their first B-17 bombing mission September 17. The 34th BGp had four Bomb Squadrons: 4th, 7th, 18th, and 391st.

Corkern and the rest of the Kennedy crew had their first bombing mission on January 14, 1945. This was in aircraft 43-38338. There will be more information about B-17 338 later.

—o-o-O-o-o—

Several types of aircraft numbers are used. These are generally known as tail numbers and the convention is to use "338338" on a vertical tail. This would indicate the aircraft was manufactured in 1943 and had military serial number 38338.

In print, this might appear as "43-38338," "338338," or "38338," and in more familiar circumstances, just "338." For aircraft manufactured in 1944, the tail number would be perhaps 46009, "44-6009."

Additionally, each aircraft had a radio call designation...in the case of 43-38338, it was B/M. "B" indicated the 18th BSq, "M" was specifically for the 43-38338 aircraft. The aircraft would often be referred to as "338 B/M".

The 4th BSq used "D" as a radio designation when the 34th was flying B-24, but after switching to B-17s, the 4th BSq became the Pathfinder Squadron for the entire 93rd Bomb Wing, and at this time assumed an "H" radio designation.

The 7th used an "E", 18th BSq a "B", and the 391st an "L". There were a few other radio call signs used in the 34th BGp because some aircraft were transferred into the 34th from other bomb groups.

—o–o–O–o–o—

January 14, Corkern and the crew had been awakened at 4 a.m. for an 8 a.m. takeoff on Mx.#112 [Mission number 112]; the aircraft were to bomb underground oil storage facilities at Derben[2], at 1:30 p.m.

Their aircraft flew in a low element of the formation. Two B-17s above them received direct hits from flak and went down northwest of Hamburg.

"We were briefed for no flak but ran into secret gun installations and lost two planes out of our lead squadron. No one got out." (JC)[3]

"Dropped bombs and fighters hit division. The G.A.F. [German Air Force] lost 180 fighters." (JC)

"On return saw P-51 knock Me-109 down west of Celle [Germany]. We lost one engine but was able to keep sight of formation and made it back OK." (RR)

An unescorted bomber lagging behind the formation with an engine problem was a "straggler." It was the common prey of the Luftwaffe and the straggler seldom survived when attacked by fighters.

The 34th had poor bombing results, but on this mission bombers and escort fighters shot down a record number of Luftwaffe fighters.

---

[2] All targets were in Germany unless otherwise noted.

[3] "(JC)" is a quote from James Corkern's mission log; "(RR)" is a quote from Roy Reid's log; the author's interjections are in brackets.

It might have been good for this new crew that their first mission was complex and not a rare "milk run."

This 39-plane sortie from the 34th BGp released 95 tons of bombs.

Many other bomb groups besides the 34th participated in these missions and many more tons of bombs were released than reported here.

—o–o–O–o–o—

The principal source of German flak (from anti-aircraft guns) was the superb 88-mm cannon. This cannon was mounted in tanks, on individual vehicles, and in network units forming anti-aircraft corridors...and these corridors could be easily moved.

The 88-mm (3-3/8-inch diameter) cannon could fire eight rounds a minute, one round every 7-1/2 seconds. It had an effective range of 46,000 feet, which was well above the altitude of the bombers. When used on the battlefield, whether mounted in a tank or as a single, standing unit, the very high muzzle velocity made the cannon deadly accurate.

The secondary anti-aircraft cannons were the 105-mm (4-1/8-inch diameter) cannons. These fired three rounds a minute with nearly the same range as the 88-mm, but the weight of the shell made its trajectory less flat and less accurate, although more damage could be done by just one round.

The anti-aircraft machine gun firing at lower flying aircraft used 37-mm shells (nearly 1-1/2-inch diameter) and fired 150 rounds a minute. Often, more than one would be mounted as a single unit. When the quad mount was used, either stationary or mobile, the firing rate was over 600 rounds a minute – 10 rounds a second. If one machine gun struck an aircraft, all four did.

Following is the entry in Roy Reid's mission logs for what was only their second mission (Mx. #114). They were flying 44-8321 B/F. Though this was only their second mission, the aircraft had already flown 28 missions.

"January 16, Tuesday, the crew took off for a mission to Bitterfeld. At about 12,000 feet over England, #3 engine almost caught fire and we had to feather engine." [Corkern wrote that the "#3 turbo ran away and we had to turn back."]

"We had to fly three hours and drop our bombs over the channel, and when we got back, weather had closed in at base.

"We found field on instruments and circled for thirty minutes trying to see runway. We were at 300 feet on three engines. It was impossible to land so we were ordered to go to Woodbridge. [Woodbridge is fifteen miles southwest of Mendlesham.] We did and landed.

"At the same time that we aborted, Jones in E (Easy) 'Old Crow' had his #3 engine catch on fire. He pulled out of formation and started bailing his crew out. We saw five men come out and chutes open and later learned that they all got out."

Corkern wrote, "However, ball turret gunner came down close to plane wreckage and concussion from explosions killed him."

Bomb group records show that "Old Crow" was B-17G, 43-38392 B/E and the pilot was W. S. Jones. All had bailed out and had chutes open, but the concussion of the plane exploding as it struck the ground collapsed the chute of the ball turret gunner, Robert Mather, and he did not survive the 150- to 200-foot fall.

—o–o–O–o–o—

For a long time, Western Europe had been a dangerous environment and there were many ways of being injured or killed.

After experiencing the dangers of taking off into complete overcast while fully loaded with bombs and fuel, the Corkern crew did not get credit for this mission...they had not crossed the battle line.

—o-o-O-o-o—

They did get credit for a second mission (Mx. #115) on January 20. The target was an oil storage area in Hamburg. Their aircraft was 43-38286.

The crew had a late takeoff but managed to merge with the formation before it departed England. One B-17 had a crash landing just after takeoff and the flight engineer and the navigator were killed when they bailed out too low. The navigator, Carlton Yarborough, Arkansas, was making his 30th mission; he would have rotated home after that one.

"Target was oil laboratories at Hamburg in the Ruhr valley, better known to us as 'Happy Valley.'" (JC)

They approached by way of Antwerp and when over the target, they started receiving heavy flak. One of 34th BGp's 32 aircraft was shot down.

The Kennedy aircraft lost power on the #1 engine, and at the same time – "a piece [of shrapnel] bounced off my helmet so we thought engine had been shot out. Thank the Lord it hit the helmet instead of me." (RR)

Corkern wrote, "We lost #1 engine first over the target but got it going again just as we lost #4. We managed to drop bombs on the target. No enemy fighters were reported.

"We had to fall out of formation over the target and make it back to England alone except for an escort of P-51s. They sure looked good to us because stragglers don't last long over Germany.

"Pieces of flak hit Roy in the head but his flak helmet saved him from injury."

Unfortunately, the prop on the bad engine could not be feathered to stop the engine's rotation. The engine was out-of-balance from flak damage so its spinning set up a heavy vibration in the wing. To make matters worse, there was a hard headwind.

Roy Reid

(Corkern photograph source)

Because of the wind and the drag from the spinning prop, fuel was being consumed too quickly. They debated going to Belgium and bailing out there rather than in the North Sea, but then decided to try to make it back to the base – or as close as they could get.

"We had to turn around and get back on course and prayed we would get back – with wing shaking as it was. We got back to England and landed with five minutes of gas supply." (RR)

"We got four flak holes today." (JC)

The flight delivered 54 tons of bombs.

On most of these missions, flak fragments might hit the aircraft at any time and these spinning, sharp pieces of steel could be one-half inch to six inches long. This shrapnel lost energy coming through the aluminum skin of the aircraft, in which case the crewmen's flak helmet, or vests could provide some protection.

Earlier, 80% of the wounds had been from shrapnel, but after the introduction of helmets and flak vests, it dropped to 32%.

—o–o–O–o–o—

On January 23, for the third mission (Mx. #116), they were in 43-38391. Oddly enough, this aircraft was manufactured immediately before "Old Crow" 43-38392, which had crashed seven days before. The rail yards at Neuss were to be bombed in direct support of ground troops. Their aircraft, carrying twelve 500-pound bombs, was in Germany only 40 minutes.

One B-17, from another bomb group, was shot down by moderate flak...but for that B-17, it didn't make any difference if they were hit by "moderate" flak or "heavy" flak. Sometimes it was called "light – but accurate – flak." This made a point in mission briefings.

"We didn't have a bit of trouble this trip. No Jerry fighters were reported but flak was quite heavy and pretty accurate for barrage. Seven ships lost engines due to flak." (JC)

"1st day with no trouble. No engine trouble." (RR)

The aircraft could be very cold – "On mission 2 [Mx. #115 - Jan. 20], I got a little frost bite on my right ear but it was fine today." (JC)

On an earlier mission, a 34th BGp ball turret gunner, Maher, received frost bite to his right foot. Another 34th BGp crewman's electrically heated suit failed and it was reported that he nearly froze. The resourceful crew put his legs in the bombsight heater.

Generally, on these missions the 34th BGp deployed approximately 39 aircraft.

Bomb reports said there were good results from the mission.

—o–o–O–o–o—

On February 3 morning, the Grant Kennedy crew flew, but James Corkern did not. Because of a bad head cold, the flight surgeon grounded him. It is not known who the ball turret gunner was for that mission.

The mission (Mx.#119) was to bomb Gestapo and other government offices in Berlin.

Roy Reid reported heavy flak... "As we approached, I wondered if this would be the last but we made it through without a scratch. It was the biggest [bombing mission] ever yet on Berlin and about two miles of the town were wiped out. We sweated out gasoline on return but made it OK and landed at 3:30."

—o–o–O–o–o—

On February 9, a bridge was to be bombed at Wensl by the request of the army; however, undercast forced the group to go to the secondary target at Dulmen. For this fourth mission (Mx. #121) the crew was in B-17G, 43-38326.

Soon after crossing the German border, the aircraft lost power to the #3 engine. They decided to continue with their group and released their bombs on target even though they were lagging behind.

Later, well back, they saw the bomber stream split, but they did not know which formation was theirs. It was nearly always fatal to be a straggler over Germany, or anywhere within range of the Luftwaffe.

At the same time, while being without the protection of the formation, they lost power to the #2 engine. At least, if two engines were going to stop, #2 and #3 (or #1 and #4) was the desired combination. They were losing altitude at 500 feet a minute while still nearly 85 miles inside Germany. (When the other crews returned home, it was thought the Kennedy crew was down somewhere inside Germany.)

At 12,000 feet, they started throwing out flak suits, ammunition, and other heavy items. They were trying to at least get out of Germany before bailing out. They cleared the German lines at only 11,000 feet but with the undercast, there was no flak.

They were now out of Germany but couldn't make it to England. They opted to try to land in Belgium.

"I really sweated that out because I hadn't had a compass from the time we left England and Kennedy had no instruments to fly though soup with. The Lord made a hole for us to come down through." (RR)

By 3 p.m. they had landed in Brussels; by 7 p.m. they were walking on Brussels' city streets.

The crew had an enjoyable time in Brussels, though none of their group spoke French and they were still in their heavy flight suits.

"We were forced down in Brussels in Belgium. Had a wonderful time but left almost immediately. I guess Lady Luck must be riding with us." (JC)   *(Corkern document)*

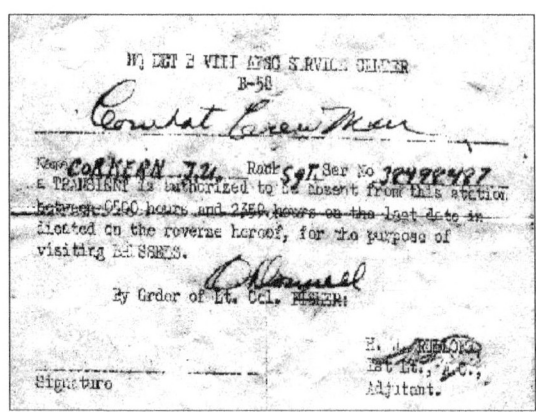

Corkern's pass from Belgium Station 58 for Brussels

The next day, they went to a training base and were flown to England in a C-47. They spent that night in Honnington, England, and returned to Mendlesham on the 11th of February.

The aircraft, 326 B/U, was not flying missions out of Mendlesham again until April 4.

—o–o–O–o–o—

While the Corkern aircraft had been lagging behind, a twin-engine British aircraft, a Mosquito, was monitoring the formation, and 34th BGp records state, "aircraft committed hostile acts by flying a pursuit curve, nearly being fired on, and almost causing an accident by giving some aircraft prop-wash."

"It was only fifth mission but got enough gray hairs for thirty. First mission with Scotty." (RR)

Their original co-pilot, Eugene Blatz, who had trained and come over to England with them, developed a nervous condition and was replaced by "Scotty" O'Brien from Fall River, Massachusetts. It would be understandable if a pilot or co-pilot developed a nervous condition.

Blatz was temporarily grounded. Reid wrote a letter to the base Flight Surgeon requesting that Blatz not be permanently removed from flight status or lose his rating.

A short time later Blatz was assigned as an observer to a squadron commander who flew lead aircraft. From the tail gunner position, Blatz watched the alignment of the formations, and by radio instructed pilots how to maintain proper formation. This contributed to both mutual protection and bombing accuracy.

This remained Blatz's position until he was reassigned as a combat aircraft co-pilot.

Eugene Blatz *(Corkern photograph source)*

—o-o-O-o-o—

It is likely that pilots and crews were not familiar with the individual aircraft they would fly on a mission. Even though an aircraft may have been "assigned" to a crew, the flight crew did not know which aircraft they would fly until the mission's morning briefing. They would be told the aircraft tail number and its hard stand location.

They arose early, worked hard in a stressful environment, and were happy to get to bed as soon as they could. There was little time for fraternization between crews other than the ones with whom they shared quarters.

The officers of three flight crews shared quarters, and nearby their enlisted crewmen quartered together.

These three crews might develop a close relationship, but the details of a particular aircraft would likely be unknown.

However, crew stories were shared and it can be assumed that Corkern heard of the recent experience of another 34th BGp ball turret gunner, 18-year-old Donald Forsman, of the 7th BSq.

During this early part of 1945, Forsman was flying a mission to Duisberg in "No Gum Chum," 416 E/C. His pilot was O'Grady and as was the custom, each gun station was tested soon after becoming airborne.

Forsman had reached back to latch the ball turret door behind him and started settling in. He applied power to the turret, hooked up his oxygen hose, plugged in his heated suit and headset, and went about doing the several other operations necessary to make the turret combat-ready. He did not use the back or seat strap because he did not want to feel unnecessarily confined in the ball turret. Other ball turret gunners expressed similar feelings.

He put his hands on the grips of the control yoke, pulled them back, and started elevating the turret from near straight down to about 45 degrees below the horizon. He pulled the "D" rings near his heels to charge the guns, put his hands back on the yoke grips and aimed at an area of unoccupied sky. He pressed the buttons at the top of the grips and fired a few rounds to confirm that the turret was operating properly.

Then Forsman moved the yoke to change elevation again.

Nothing happened.

He moved the yoke the opposite direction.

Still nothing moved.

He tried changing the elevation manually with the hand crank located above his left shoulder.

It would not move either direction.

The crew was notified that he had no control of elevation.

A crewmember put the hand crank on the elevation gearbox shaft that was available in the fuselage. This shaft had a square end to interface with the crank and it protruded vertically from the right side of the large azimuth ring. It could not be turned.

Forsman was a prisoner in the turret. This was every ball turret gunner's fear.

Even if the aircraft landed properly, the gun barrels of the two heavy guns would strike the landing surface. The guns could break loose and thrash around inside the turret. The gunner's head was within inches of both guns.

Pilot O'Grady asked Forsman if they should abort the mission. He said to continue.

Though the target was only 20 miles inside Germany, it was in the Ruhr Valley near Essen and Dusseldorf, and heavily defended by flak batteries. If the aircraft was badly damaged, eight crewmen would have options; Forsman would have none.

Of the ten 34th BGp bombers arriving over the target, eight received damage; two received major damage. However, there was no damage to the O'Grady 326 B/U with Forsman trapped in the turret.

After leaving the target area, their attention could turn to getting Forsman free before they had to land.

O'Grady started circling over the English coast while the crew removed a barrel from a .50 caliber machine gun and started beating on the turret mechanism. They had to beat through aluminum to force an opening to the elevation sector gear drive. This was shielded by the azimuth ring.

The aluminum azimuth ring was the major ball turret structure and was mounted to the aircraft floor. It was a larger diameter than the turret and gear teeth (nearly 1/2" thick) were around the inside circumference.

The rest of the aluminum ball structure was thick, cast aluminum.

As one crewman got tired, another would take his place until eventually they managed to break off enough teeth and structure for the gun barrel to reach the elevation sector gear mechanism.

Finally, the area was sufficiently broken away so the turret's position could be manually elevated to permit the hatch door to be opened and Forsman set free. He had been trapped in the turret for four hours.[4]

Ball turret gunners were exposed to unique risks.

—o–o–O–o–o—

On Valentine's Day, 1945, they were awakened at 2:30 a.m. and were briefed an hour later. The crew was back in 43-38338 and Chemnitz was the target (Mx. #122). "...bomb a bridge at a small town just south of Berlin. Mostly to help Russians." (JC)

They approached the target by way of Frankfurt, where they experienced flak; at Chemnitz there was light flak. A part of the group did not bomb Chemnitz but chose a target of opportunity, Sonnenberg.

---

[4] This event is described in "The American Airman in Europe" (Roger A. Freeman) but that account was provided by the navigator. The account presented here is from conversations between the author and Donald Forsman himself and it differs on several points.

No fighters hit us but I saw a couple of dog fights by our escort We didn't lose any of our engines today. It was mostly a milk run but we came out through 'Happy Valley.'" (JC)

They released 5,000 pounds of bombs and saw the bombs of a lower element hit the marshaling yards. There was some flak on their flight back. They landed at 4:45 p.m. Considering the time for deplaning and debriefing, this was another long day.

These days started very early and while some crewmen had breakfast, others were in briefings. For breakfast, Roy Reid would occasionally have someone bring him an egg sandwich from the mess hall. He would eat it whenever he found time before takeoff.

Each crewmember was responsible for what he would eat during the mission, if anything. For Reid it was often a candy bar, which he would eat en route back to the base. However, the candy might have become very cold. Once the low temperature made a candy bar with nougat particularly tenacious and Reid lost a filling to it.

The crew usually took hard candy in case they had to bail out over unfriendly territory. They also had money and a map. Because their flight boots were not comfortable for general walking, Reid wired a pair of shoes to his parachute, just in case.

Navigator station (similar to that of Reid's) is on left side of aircraft just forward of flight deck. Windows align with engines; similar windows are on right side. Out of the photograph to the right is a clear view forward through nose glazing. Straight overhead is the astrodome

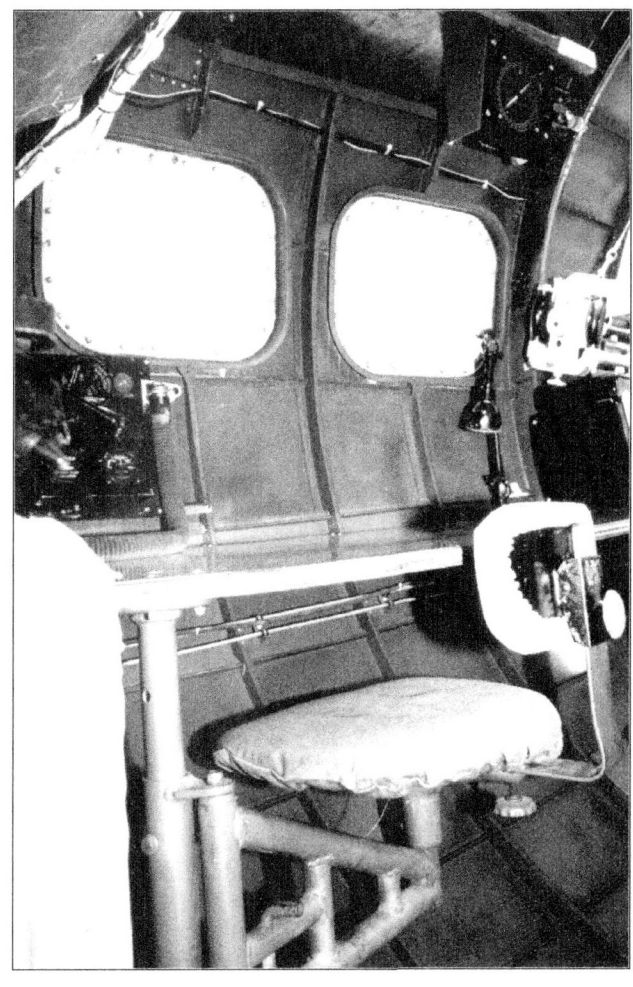

(Cashion photograph)

for astronomical sightings.

Upper right of photograph is indicator for external, directional antenna position. Articulating map light is secured to work surface just below breech of left cheek machine gun. Wooden ammo box for that gun would sometimes mount where lamp is.

Swiveling seat is adjustable.

Left center is radio compass control panel. Clipped to top right corner of that panel is the end of the oxygen hose for the mask. The clip would be removed and secured to strap on crewmember and the short oxygen mask hose would be connected

into that. Oxygen regulator, pressure gauge, and flow meter are out of photograph immediately left of radio compass panel, as is the radio/intercom control box.

The morning of February 15, they were awakened at 3 a.m. for Mx.#123. This would be a mission to a synthetic oil plant near Cottbus, 60 miles southeast of Berlin.

At 7 a.m., they were airborne in their seventh B-17 in as many missions; this time it was 44-6840.

The primary target was overcast so they continued to the secondary target of Cottbus-proper where they experienced meager flak.

The number of anti-aircraft guns occupying some defined area determined whether flak was considered light, medium, heavy, or some other description. In this case, it was estimated that there were 30 anti-aircraft guns. This was considered meager.

The Kennedy aircraft was over the target at 12:30 and then started back to England by way of South Koblenz.

The radioman's compartment was just aft of the bomb bay and it was common that after bombs were released, the radioman opened the door between his compartment and the bomb bay to confirm that all bombs were free of the aircraft.

This time there were still some bombs hanging in the racks.

On occasion the release gate did not clear the shackle at the top of the bomb and these fixtures became wedged. A hard shove with a foot could swing the bomb enough that it would release. Hung-up bombs were not unusual; kicking them loose was common.

A gunner, Paul Thomas, came forward from the waist and kicked them loose.

The crew arrived back at the airbase at 3:30 p.m.; they had been over Germany for well over five hours.

"The mission was 9 hrs. and 10 mins. long." (JC)

One aircraft had been lost with the nine crewmen MIA.

Back row, left to right -- Assist. Engineer/Gunner Cleo Baughman; Engineer/Gunner Everette Riggs; Tail Gunner James Ballard; Co-pilot Eward O'Brien; Pilot Grant Kennedy; Navigator Roy Reid.

Front row, left to right -- Tail Gunner Len Muellerleile; Gunner Paul Thomas; Ball Turret Gunner James Corkern; Radioman/Gunner Roger Erickson. *The crew is posing with B-17G 44-6960, a bomber they never flew. This aircraft flew no mission with the 34th BGp though it is showing a 34th BGp "H" in the red over- paint on the vertical tail. The aircraft returned to the US after the* *war. Muellerleile is shown in other photographs as a tail gunner, but there is no record of his flying with this crew. Their bombardier, Kenneth Kessinger, is not present.*

(Corkern photograph source)

They were awakened at 3:30 a.m., February 17, and briefed to go to Cottbus again (Mx. #124). For the next two missions, they would remain in 44-6840.

While still over France, they were informed that there were weather problems at the target and they were directed to Frankfurt, 270 miles southwest of Cottbus.

They experienced meager flak crossing the battle line, partially because their aircraft was division lead and the anti-aircraft gunners had not "zeroed in" on the formations.

The bomb run was from the northwest and they continued southeast to the rallying point before making a turn for the flight home. But again, there were hung-up bombs as on the previous mission with this same aircraft.

The aircraft pulled from the formation (always hazardous) so they could try to free the bombs one at a time. There were several small German towns en route back to their base so they would try to drop the bombs on them.

One bomb hit a road, one landed at the edge of a town, and one landed in the center of a small town. They were carrying ten 500-pound bombs.

B-17s from other groups had been shot down by flak.

—o–o–O–o–o—

On February 20, after being aroused at 3 a.m., they were briefed on bombing marshaling yards at Nurnberg (Mx. #126).

The flight approached the target by way of Ostend, Brussels, and Strasbourg.

Starting at the channel, the weather was so thick there were times they could not see all the bombers in their own squadron. They were supposed to bomb from 24,000 feet, but weather forced them higher. They approached from the south and released bombs by instruments. Flak was moderate-to-heavy with an estimate of 140 anti-aircraft guns.

"Plenty of flak but it wasn't accurate today. We had four good engines. It was a long haul." (JC)

The departure route was the reverse of the arrival route. The formation started descending through the weather at Strasbourg and flew in bad weather all the way to England.

"We got no holes but sure thought we would. The good Lord was with us and here is hoping that he continues...one less to go." (RR)

This time 44-6840 released all bombs. The group had delivered 87 tons of bombs.

—o–o–O–o–o—

For the first time, on February 21, they flew in 43-38409. This was a return mission (Mx. #127) to Nurnberg marshaling yards where there were "unusual things" in the rail yards, on which the 34th BGp delivered 85 tons of bombs. The Kennedy B-17 released ten 500-pound bombs.

Flak over the target was reported to be thick enough to walk on; estimate was still 140 guns. The aircraft received 11 hits but no lasting damage. They got a hole in a fuel tank from flak fragments.

"There was plenty of flak and it was accurate. We got at least ten holes but everyone returned safe. A piece hit my B.T. [Ball Turret] glass and broke it. Good thing it is bullet proof. Had four good engines." (JC)

One B-17 had the hydraulic system shot out and landed wheels-up on grass back at the base.

Flying in another B-17, Eugene Blatz, the original Kennedy crew co-pilot, had his chute harness cut by shrapnel, and his aircraft received such damage that the entire tail section needed replacement.

Corkern and crew landed at 3:10 p.m.

Returning to bomb the marshaling yards the second day was supposed to have been a surprise for the Germans... "but it turned out so that the surprise was on us...a rough day I would say." (RR)

It was just another 12-hour day for an 8th AAF bomber crew.

Map of Germany showing crew's bombing missions from January 14 through April 16, 1945.

Not shown are Missions #164, #165, and #166; all on French coast.

The location of Mission #137 is undetermined but thought to be near Dortmund.

Also not shown is Mission #119 to Berlin. This was flown by the Kennedy crew but without Corkern who was ill that day.

Spellings of the mission target names were current for 1945.

—o-o-O-o-o—

Chapter V

A Crew of Pros

By the last week of February, the crew had earned some quality rest. They enjoyed their leisure time in different ways. Some stayed near the base or made day trips. Roy Reid went to London to enjoy restaurant meals and see part of the city.

The first of March, the crew was awakened at 4 a.m., and then in yet another B-17, 44-8209, they took off to bomb marshaling yards at Ulm. This would be Mx. #133.

The route into Germany went over Ostend, Luxembourg, Strasbourg, and then to an area northwest of Ulm where they started their bomb approach.

The visibility was poor so they relied on instruments to align on the target. They were just one of the 37 bombers from the 34th BGp which delivered 117 tons of bombs. This mission would take nine hours and cover 1,200 round-trip miles.

While crossing the enemy lines on the flight out of Germany, there was light but accurate flak. "Hemingway and a few others got hits and holes but no one wounded. Results were not so good I don't think, however, we didn't see the ground." (RR)

"Target was marshaling yards at Ulm. It was a long haul but not much flak. The crew is still together." (JC)

—o‑o‑O‑o‑o—

By this time, Corkern personally knew many of the other aircraft crewmen. He had seen enough combat and heard a lot of stories; his concern for the welfare of his crewmates warranted a comment in his mission log. This will become a closing statement on almost all of his future missions.

March 2 marked a change for the 34th BGp. For this raid, the target was to be bombed by visual contact only, but weather forced them to their secondary target of Dresden town center. They were in B-17G 43-38216.

Just before reaching the initial point where the bomb approach started northwest of Dresden, the formation ahead of Corkern's crew was attacked by fighters.

—o–o–O–o–o—

For nearly ten months, the 34th BGp had not been attacked by the Luftwaffe. There could be several reasons for this but one is that the 34th pilots flew very tight formations.

Attacking fighters, given a choice between a tightly packed formation and one more open, would attack the open one.

It was noted in a few log entries that the groups ahead or behind the 34th were attacked when the 34th BGp was not. Combat veterans of the 34th with whom the author has spoken credit bomber piloting skills for helping discourage fighter attacks.

Luftwaffe fighters would attack the last bomber, or one flying well out on a flank. They really preferred a lone straggler trying to get home on three engines.

—o–o–O–o–o—

By this time in the European air war, there were US fighter pilots who said they could look from horizon to horizon and see a constant stream of bombers flying toward Germany. A few miles to one side or the other would be another stream on its way back to England.

There were many escort fighters but they had a lot of sky to defend.

During this March 2 mission, the bombers' escort fighters had been called from the front of the bomber stream to the rear where German fighters were attacking. This was a ploy to strip escorts from the front. The distance from the front to the rear of an individual mission stream could be many miles.

As soon as the escort fighters were engaged at the rear, as many as 35 Me-262 jets attacked the leading formations from all levels and all directions.

It was 10:17 and the jets, attacking in groups of three, immediately shot nine B-17s (81 - 90 crewmen) out of the formation. Two of the ships had engine fires, and passed near the Kennedy aircraft; the crew saw them explode and disintegrate.

The lead aircraft of their formation had waist gunner, John Frey, killed, and its pilot, Z. Richardson, wounded. This B-17 and one other had to land in Belgium. Altogether, 14 B-17s were badly damaged.

The Kennedy crew made their bomb run with three types of German fighters thick in the sky. Just as they reached the rallying point to reassemble for the turn home, German fighters swarmed the 34th BGp squadrons.

Few American fighters carried anything other than .50 caliber machine guns (1/2-inch diameter) and while these were very effective weapons, firing 750 rounds a minute, they did not have exploding shells as a cannon did.

Luftwaffe fighters had cannons as well as machine guns. The machine guns were either 13-mm (1/2-inch diameter) or 20-mm (3/4-inch diameter). They had a similar range of 3,600 feet; the 13-mm fired 900 rounds a minute, and the 20-mm a little less. The FW-190s carried four 20-mm machine guns, plus cannons.

Most of the German fighters had two MK108 30-mm (near 1-1/8-inch diameter) cannons. These fired 600 rounds a minute and were on Me-109s. Four similar cannons were on the FW-190. Though they had an effective range of only 750 feet, five hits would destroy a four-engine bomber.

Four cannons were in the nose of the Me-262 jet and each cannon fired 600 rounds a minute. With their ability to easily overtake a bomber, a lot of damage could be done to a formation and its crews.

Some of their incendiary cannon shells had fuzes which would only explode when striking fluids – such as fuel.

—o–o–O–o–o—

Corkern's aircraft was flying the dangerous Tail-End-Charlie position and they were about to lose an engine. With the sagging engine, they were at risk of falling dangerously behind. They did not want to become a "straggler"; a generally doomed position when the Luftwaffe was in the area.

Two Me-109s started turning to attack Corkern's aircraft. One turned away, but the other completed its attack and passed under the left wing.

Then an FW-190 prepared to attack from the left. He was climbing to their altitude and as he completed his climb, he started turning toward them. Just then he received hits from another bomber, started down, and caught fire.

As long as a B-17 could stay in a tight formation, the combined overlapping defensive firepower was considerable.

"The P-51s had their hands full but they did a good job." (RR)

"P-51 got 66 Jerries in the air and 38 on the ground!" (JC)

After nearly 20 minutes, the Luftwaffe broke off the attack; the jets had only a maximum of 10 seconds of ammunition and the Me-109 cannons fired for only 8 seconds. It was also fortunate that the Me-262 cannons were prone to jamming.

B-17s "Butch," "Ol'Buddy," and "Sweet Seventeen" had gunners claiming a total of eight fighters destroyed, seven probable, and eight damaged.

Bomb group records indicate that engineer/top turret gunner, Lombard, flying with the Kennedy crew, was credited with one aircraft damaged.

"How we got through, I don't know. The good Lord brought us through and believe me, I thanked him. Hope I don't see any more of those." (RR)

"I was scared. The crew is still together." (JC)

News reports that day said that 129 Luftwaffe fighters had been shot down.

—o–o–O–o–o—

When the Corkern crew members had shipped out for England in November, 1944, the original engineer/top turret gunner, Everette Riggs, had been confined in a hospital, so another engineer/gunner, Michael Lombard, was assigned to the Kennedy crew.

The 34th BGp records list the engineer as "Lombard," yet later, he was known to crew members as "Lombardi." It is Lombard who is referred to as "Mick" or "Mickey" in mission logs.

Though Everette Riggs came to England later, Lombard continued flying until the assistant engineer/gunner, Cleo Baughman, could qualify for a full, flight engineer rating.

Just as Eugene Blatz continued with the group after O'Brien had taken his place on the crew, Riggs's association continued after Lombard joined the crew.

—o–o–O–o–o—

On March 3, back in 43-38409 for Mx. #135, they tried to bomb an underground oil storage facility near Celle, but were directed to continue to the secondary target of Hildesheim.

Just as the lead aircraft bombardier had the bombsight aligned on the target and was preparing to release the bombs (which would signal all the formation to release theirs), another flight of B-17s moved across the bombsight's field-of-view. These bombers were releasing their bombs from a lower altitude.

The lead aircraft of the 34th's formation had almost released the formation's bombs on B-17s on another mission.

This mission demonstrates changes in target priorities and it gives an indication of the mass of bombers over Germany at this time. One mission's secondary target might be another mission's target of last resort.

—o–o–O–o–o—

The 34th BGp and the other bomb groups of this mission then moved to their target of last resort, Bielefeld. They made an instrument approach, released their bombs, and started their descent for England and the comfort of their home base.

"No flak was close but we saw a damn good dog fight behind us. No fighters attacked us today. Hope the luck holds out. The crew is still together. I am pretty tired. Probably fly tomorrow." (JC)

This had become a long mission for them, but not for a B-17 in another bomb group – jets caught it near Reims, France, and the B-17 went down burning.

On March 4, the target for Mx. #136 was Nurnburg. The crews were out of their bunks at 3 a.m. and made a 6:50 a.m. takeoff. The flight went to Reims, France, to assemble for the mission. The Corkern aircrew, again flying 43-38409, tried to locate the formation but they were at the wrong place.

About 10 minutes before they crossed the battle line, the crew caught up with the formation and moved into the proper position. Almost immediately the mission was recalled.

On the way back, the formations were fired on by flak and some aircraft were hit; however, no shrapnel struck Corkern's aircraft.

The mission was not without a serious loss, however. It is fortunate that the Corkern crew was not in aircraft 43-38338 B/M again. During assembly over France, there was a mid-air collision between 338 B/M and 43-39071 B/K, both from Corkern's 18th BSq.

In bad weather, one came down into the other and the lower aircraft lost its tail. Half of its wing exploded and the two sections fell separately. The upper aircraft lost its wing tip and spun out of control into the clouds. Only one parachute was seen.

Pilot Parson and his crew in 071 B/K were killed; pilot Mueller and seven of his crew were killed in 338 B/M. The tail gunner, Kippen, though wounded, was the lone survivor; it was his parachute that was seen.

"I forgot what the target was but we didn't get to go there because clouds were too high. We went over the battle lines and got flak and had to return on account of weather. We brought our bombs back but got credit for a mission. Two planes were lost due to weather and collision. One of our good buddies was in the crash. I sure did hate it." (JC)

This mission and date were confused in Corkern's mission log so the date and mission number have been corrected to make his comments relevant.

Such confusion in personal logs is understandable...and common. No doubt a crew gunner knew basically where he was and when he was there, but after-the-fact entries, made when very tired and about things where there had been much anxiety may not be recalled in great detail or accuracy later.

There are now apparent inconsistencies in reports compiled at the time of the missions, but they no doubt were correct and understood then.

It is only now, more than half a century later, that they are difficult to merge; particularly when they involve personal logs of two crewmembers, bomb group records, records kept by the bomb squadron, conversations with crewmen, and data from miscellaneous notes and charts found in various publications.

Autographed paper money was a common keepsake for aircrews. Corkern's two dollar bill was signed by:

Paul N. Thomas

Everette P. Riggs

Roy L. Reid
James L. Ballard
Hurricane, Utah

Cleo J. Baughman
Stockton, Kansas
Grant Kennedy
Star Lake, NY
Eugene Blatz

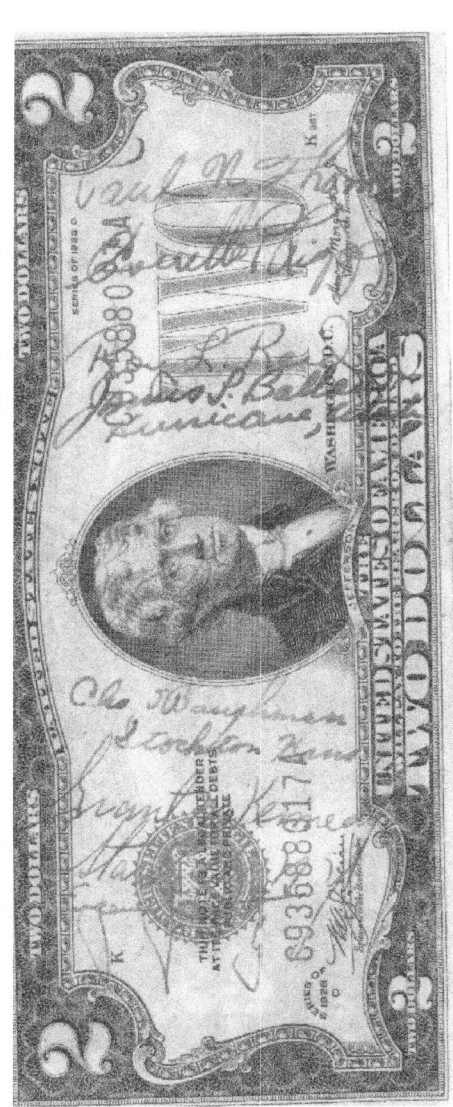

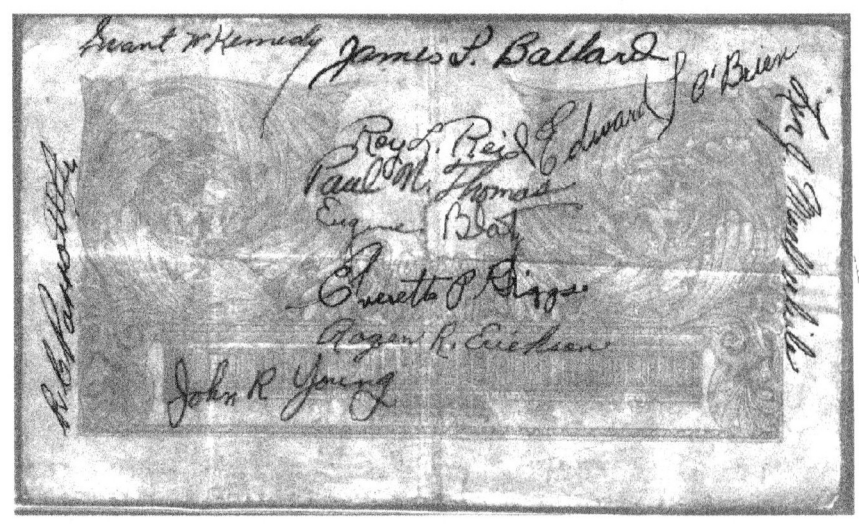

Corkern's one pound note was signed by:

Grant W. Kennedy   **James Ballard**
                          Roy Reid   **Edward O'Brien**
                          Paul Thomas
                          Eugene Blatz
                          Everette Riggs
                          Roger R. Erickson
       John Young
R. G. Parrotti, Jr. (?)   **Len J. Muellerleile**

**Michael
Lombard**

Mx. #137, on March 7, was a 44-bomber sortie to a synthetic fuel (Benzoil) plant at Dattlen, near Dortmund. This was a return to "Happy Valley" and while six aircraft released chaff, other 34th BGp aircraft delivered 125 tons of bombs.

For the first time, the Corkern crew was in aircraft 43-37960; they released twelve 500- pound bombs. This target was supposed to have been bombed visually, but the target had 80% cloud cover so it was bombed by instruments.

The flak was moderate but the aircraft received no holes and the mission formation lost no aircraft.

"It was easy mission if there be such a thing." (RR)

This was aircraft 43-37960's first mission, and the aircraft will become important to Corkern, Reid, and crew.

—o–o–O–o–o—

On March 10, they flew Mx. #139 to Soest, "Happy Valley," to bomb marshaling yards just east of Dortmund. These railways were being used to ship material to the Western Front.

Except for a portion of Holland, the cloud coverage was near 100% so the bomb approach was made by instruments. Flak was light and none of the bomb group aircraft received holes.

"We didn't get any fighters or flak holes. We carried leaflets and money and ration points but the rest of the group carried 42-100 pounders. We have been assigned a new ship. No. 960 L - for Love." (JC)

—o–o–O–o–o—

This was B-17G-75-BO, 43-37960, and the radio call sign was "960 B/L."

For this mission, the crew radio operator, Roger Erickson, was left behind and Jack Share took his place. This was Jack Share's first mission.

Eighty-seven tons of bombs were delivered by the group; three tons by Corkern's crew in 43-37960, according to navigator Roy Reid's mission log.

—o-o-O-o-o—

The Kennedy crew was a backup crew for Mx.#142, March 14. They would be awakened with the other crews and be prepared to fly. At the briefing, it would be determined if all the assigned crews were present and ready to fly. If so, the unneeded crew could stand down, and it's likely that most of them would go back to bed.

If one of the aircraft developed difficulties before takeoff, it was a real-time decision whether the crew would move to a standby aircraft or stand down. These standby aircraft, without assigned crews, would have been prepared for the mission just as the other mission aircraft were.

—o-o-O-o-o—

The bomb group continued to focus on marshaling yards, and on March 15, Mx. #143, the target was the railway complex at Oranienburg (20 miles northeast of Berlin). The crew was permitted to sleep until 5:30 a.m. and the takeoff was a late 11 a.m. The visibility was good to and from the target.

The specific targets were troops and materiel being moved from the Eastern to the Western Front.

Flak was moderate on approach and none of the aircraft received holes, but on departure, light (but accurate) flak around Wittenburg did hit some of the aircraft.

—o-o-O-o-o—

"We got flak from Berlin and just about every other place. We ran into some secret flak guns but didn't lose any planes. I sure do like our new plane [960 B/L]. The crew is still together. We didn't get any [German] fighters today." (JC)

The target received 110 tons of bombs and these were particularly dangerous bombs. 960 B/L was carrying twelve 500-pound bombs and the bomb fuzes were set to detonate anytime from the instant of impact to as many as six days later!

Landing was at 6:30 pm.

The mission covered 1,350 miles.

—o-o-O-o-o—

Mx. #144 was to Bitterfeld on March 17. The crew was awakened at 4 a.m. and took off at 8 a.m. in their 960 B/L.

The formations flew through thick clouds for half the flight and it was necessary to approach the target 4,000 feet higher than the briefed altitude. The temperature was minus 53 degrees F.

They approached the target by way of Antwerp, Frankfurt, and Chemnitz. The weather was so bad that the 7th BSq was lost on the way and never found the formation before they reached the target – they had been 50 miles off course.

The departure from Germany was to be the same route as the approach, but part of the formation was carried off-course near Frankfurt and was fired on by flak units. Four of the five bombers were hit, including six or seven hits on 960 B/L.

One hole in 960 B/L was large enough to put a fist through.

"Ball turret oxygen line shot out, CO-2 bottle hit beside co-pilot, rear door knocked shut, and light wiring cut." (RR)

"There was no flak on the target but we got some after leaving the target. All close calls. I had my oxygen line cut and some wires. Cleo [Baughman] had a close one, too, and Mick's was real close. Everyone returned safe." (JC)

Two ships from the 490th BGp had mid-air over France.

The bomb group landed back at Mendlesham near 4:30 after a 1,300-mile mission.

For the March 18 Mx. #145, the crew slept until 6 a.m. and then was briefed for an 11 a.m. takeoff. There was cloud coverage all the way to Berlin. The sky cleared over the target; armament factories and the city were plainly visible. The 38-bomber sortie delivered 95 tons of bombs and a large number of fires were caused by the incendiaries. There was smoke to 18,000 feet.

Flak was moderate-to-heavy and Myers' aircraft from Corkern's 18th BSq was hit.

Myers flew the damaged B-17, "Old Times" (43-38912 B/I), east until they were behind Russian lines in Poland and made a forced landing. The crew was MIA. (The aircraft was subsequently salvaged but it was two months before Myers was back piloting a B-17.)

Reid reported, "We didn't get but two or three holes. Lucky again!"

Reid also reported that they were carrying both high explosive bombs and incendiaries. It is assumed that "they" meant their aircraft and not the bomb group in general.

There is confusion in the logs for this mission. When correlating multiple logs and bomb group mission reports, there will be some entries which remain unclear.

Bomb group records state that 960 B/L with pilot Kennedy was carrying leaflets only.

"Target was Berlin and we really tore the hell out of it. Flak was pretty heavy but we only got one hole. Almost had to land in Russia." (JC)

The author discussed this mission with Roy Reid and he had no recollections of any serious damage or discussions about diverting to Russia. As navigator, he would have been involved in the discussions and this is something he would likely remember.

Bomb group records report that two B-17s were heavily damaged but these were bombers from a squadron other than the 18 BSq.

It is not known if Corkern ever flew with another crew.

—o–o–O–o–o—

The next day (March 19), they flew Mx. #146 and the target was a 32-gun flak battery at Merseberg. The crew was still in 960 B/L and the target was to be bombed visually only. This was one of the toughest targets in Germany and the crews started worrying as soon as the briefing maps were uncovered and they saw their target.

Before getting to the target "the good Lord came to our rescue and provided cloud coverage and we were forced to go to secondary target." (RR)

This target was a precision instrument factory in Jena. The city was known for its superb optics and instrumentation industries, including an important Zeiss lens factory.

Reid reported that Corkern saw several bombs hit in a pasture near the target, so it seems that some or all of their bombs missed. But the contrails had been very bad and it was difficult to see from their altitude. In the bad weather, they even lost sight of their formation while in a turn.

"The flak wasn't too heavy and no fighter attacks. We got one hole. One ship had #1 engine blown off but got back. The crew is still together." (JC)

Bomb group records indicate only minor engine or turbo charger problems in three aircraft but no battle damage to any 34th BGp aircraft so the B-17 having an engine blown away had to be in another bomb group.

—o–o–O–o–o—

On March 21, 960 B/L was flown on Mx. #148 to an airfield complex in Marx near Rustringen. The target was supposed to be bombed visually and their entrance was to be by way of the North Sea. This was over an unknown flak corridor. Fortunately, there was no flak.

The lead bombardier was very accurate and they "plastered the field. Each group took a different airfield and all did a good job. We carried propaganda leaflets." (RR) [Underline is RR's.]

The 34th BGp had 37 aircraft on the mission delivering 129 tons of bombs.

As they were leaving the area, they saw RAF bombers arriving, "Which was scattered all over the sky and looked like a swarm of bees. There had been good weather and no flak. If there is such a thing as a 'milk run,' this turned out to be one, but of course, there isn't." (RR)

What might be a "milk run" for one aircraft crew could be dangerous for another. Even on this "milk run," one aircraft had to crash-land in Britain.

—o-o-O-o-o—

The next day, March 22, they slept until nearly 9:30 a.m. and were briefed to bomb German Headquarters at Ratingen, Germany, just beyond the Rhine River. This mission, Mx. #149, was only five miles into "Happy Valley."

Bombing in "visual-only" conditions meant very few clouds or overcast, and this meant that the flak batteries could see the bombers as well as the bombers could see the ground. The flak in this case was heavy and some aircraft were hit, but 960 B/L received only one hole.

"Target today were German troops at Ratingen. We got excellent results. The flak wasn't too bad but there was plenty. The crew is still together with the exception of Mick." (JC)

"One of the shortest mission I ever flew...4-1/2 hours long." (RR)

The target received 105 tons of bombs from the bomb group.

It can be assumed that it was near this time that Cleo Baughman received his full, flight engineer rating, allowing Michael Lombard to fly with other crews.

34th BGp B-17s on a bombing mission.

(Corkern photograph source)

For Mx. #150 on March 23, the target was Geisecke marshaling yard, and this was to be a costly mission. The crew had had only one day off in the last seven.

They had flown to the initial point through Kablenze and approached the target from the south.

The ground war on the Western Front was approaching the Rhine and as the formation went over, US artillery was shelling the flak batteries.

Bomb group records state that circumstances had the 34th BGp bomb path on a collision course with the bomb path of a 447th BGp formation. Just as 34th BGp B-17 43-38971 B/A, piloted by Myron Bolser, released its bombs and started an evasive turn to the left, its left wing was hit by flak. The shell blew off three or four feet of the wing tip.

The loss of lift on the left side and the increased drag on the distorted left wing forced the aircraft to turn to the left even more. The subsequent loss of altitude caused the aircraft to collide with a B-17 from another bomb group.

That B-17 was one of a three-plane element on a collision course with the 34th BGp flight and it, too, had initiated an evasive turn.

Two crewmen were seen coming from the collision – one with parachute; one without. There were no survivors on the Bolser aircraft which was from the 18th BSq, the same as Corkern's.

The bomb group delivered 81 tons of bombs, displaced train rails, and started numerous fires; one, a large oil fire.

Each bomb group had hit different rail yards and there was fire and smoke scattered over a 50-mile radius. "This was known as 'softening up the Rhine'." (RR)

"This was a pretty rough mission. Not much flak but it was accurate. We lost two planes. This looks like the beginning of something big." (JC)

—o–o–O–o–o—

The Kennedy fight crew was not on the flight list the night of March 23 and would stand down the next day. However, the navigator, Roy Reid, was scheduled to fly.

B-17 960 B/L would be flown on Mx. #151, March 24, by another crew. The pilot was James Sykes from the 34th BGp's 391st BSq. Reid would fly as his navigator.

Reid was awakened at 2 a.m. and he later wrote that he was so tired, he was walking in his sleep. Because of the big US offensive east of the Rhine, they were scheduled to fly two missions that day.

The target was Oldenburg airfield. They made their visual bomb run from the south and hit the target in the center.

On the return flight there was light flak but they sustained no holes. As they left the continent over northern Holland, they were fired on from the Frisian Islands.

There were several enemy areas that had long since been cut off, but these pockets of resistance could still cause trouble. Besides the Frisian Islands, there were Dunkerque and a few coastal gun emplacements in France.

The second mission for that day was scrubbed – much to the satisfaction of the crews.

—o-o-O-o-o—

The next day, March 25, the Kennedy crew was not scheduled to fly but there was a continuation of the previous day's mission. Shortly after takeoff, the mission was canceled because of existing bad weather and the likelihood the weather would worsen before the aircrafts' return.

One of these aircraft was piloted by Lester Bennett. He and his crew were one of the other two flight crews sharing quarters with the Kennedy crew.

Bennett and crew had taken off in 44-8605 B/H and in the bad weather started climbing toward the staging area. During this crowded period of converging aircraft, Bennett, to avoid a collision, pulled the nose of his aircraft up; it stalled, lowered a wing, and started spinning.

A B-17 could recover from a stall and spin, but it required a lot of altitude; altitude Bennett did not have – they were at 6,000 feet.

The aircraft spun in and eight were killed; the co-pilot, Henry Karger, died the next day.[5]

It was bad enough for an aircrew to lose friends but to lose a crew with whom they shared quarters was worse because of the necessity of collecting and removing that crew's personal items to be sent home.

James Corkern, ball turret gunner and James Ballard, tail gunner. *(Corkern photograph source)*

—o‑o‑O‑o‑o—

5

There have been other published accounts of this accident but they differ slightly in detail.

The above account is consistent with 34th BGp records and conversations with Roy Reid. The crew consisted of Bennett, Karger, Louis Bertino (N), Kenneth Lewman (B), Roger Dilley (R), Ocko Pickett (E), Ralph Verman (BT), William Johnson (WG), and Chester Kordas (TG). Bennett and Johnson are buried at Cambridge American Cemetery, locations A-1-26 and A-6-16, respectively.

Chapter VI

Jet Attack

The next mission for the Kennedy crew was on March 30.

This mission for 960 B/L, Corkern and crew, turned particularly bad. This was Mx. #154 to submarine pens northwest of Hamburg. They were awakened at 5 a.m. and airborne at 10:30.

They approached the target from the west and received a lot of flak from 180 to 280 anti-aircraft cannons. Reid reported that one 34th BGp B-17's navigator, Danto, received flak wounds in his feet, and bomb group records indicate that an 18th BSq ball turret gunner was wounded.

After the bombs were released, the formations turned north.

About five minutes later, Me-262 jets approached the formations from the rear. A B-17 in a high squadron received hits from a jet's cannon and lost one-third of its left wing. A single exploding cannon shell from a fighter could break a wing spar.

Ballard, the tail gunner of 960 B/L, saw a jet approaching but could not fire on it because of the position of the following B-17.

The Me-262 came straight for 960 B/L and cannon shells struck their tail section. The explosions blew off all but a foot from the left elevator. This removed a third of the left horizontal tail area and half of Kennedy's ability to control aircraft pitch.

The explosions spread shrapnel throughout the tail section. An oxygen line was severed and some control cables were hit, but fortunately not cut through.

Twelve pieces of shrapnel hit Ballard's armor plating but only one piece penetrated. Miraculously, no one was wounded.

"We got back at 8 p.m." (RR)

The tail had been badly damaged "making about 300 holes. The tail section actually looked like a sieve." (RR)

Corkern reported, "Fighters hit us today. They were 262 jet jobs and they shot almost all of our tail off. 300 holes. You can't beat a 17 for coming back shot up. Rough mission. The crew is still together." (JC)

Corkern's comments are dated the previous day, but there was no mission that day and the events described in his log correspond with this mission.

They crew had dropped no bombs – only leaflets.

—o–o–O–o–o—

The next day, March 31 (Mx. #155), 960 B/L did not fly. It can be assumed that it was receiving major tail assembly repair from cannibalized aircraft. Instead of 960 B/L, the crew was in 44-6929. The mission was to an underground gasoline storage complex near Leipzig.

They were airborne at 6 a.m. and approached the target by way of North Koblenz, and then east and northeast toward Leipzig. The weather at Leipzig was unfavorable for visual bombing so the mission continued to an area 30 miles west. This was the initial point to begin their bomb run on an armored car factory in Brandenburg.

"The flak wasn't too bad. The clouds and haze was rough. No Jerry fighters came up. Hope they stay down. I have seen enough of them. The crew is still together." (JC)

Their aircraft received no hits; however, near Halberstadt, a B-17 in another group was hit by flak and "it disintegrated in the air. It left nothing but a puff of oil smoke in the air." (RR)

—o–o–O–o–o—

After a couple of days of rest, on April 3, they were back in 960 B/L for Mx. #156. They had been awakened at 2 a.m. and were briefed to destroy a German naval fleet. The Russians had taken control of Konisberg and Danzig so German ships were being serviced in Kiel.

When the crew got to the aircraft, they were told to go back to bed.

They were awakened again at 10 a.m. and took off at 1 p.m.[6]

Going by way of the North Sea, the B-17 formations arrived over Kiel near 5:30 p.m. The overcast had closed in so the bomb approach was by instruments. There was moderate flak but 960 B/L received no hits.

"The flak wasn't too bad but you could see the fire when it exploded." (JC)

As they departed to the east and made a turn over the Baltic Sea, they saw a large number of German naval vessels leaving the harbor.

"No fighters opposed us. I sure hope they stay down after last trip." (JC) [Meaning "the last trip" in 960 B/L.]

The bombers had started arriving back at Mendlesham at 8:30 p.m. and debriefing kept the crew from getting to bed until near 11 p.m., "knowing it would be early rise next morning." (RR)

—o-o-O-o-o—

Reid was correct. They were awake by 2:45 a.m. and in the briefing rooms at 4. And "again it was Kiel, to our disappointment, but of course we had no choice." (RR)

---

[6]

Although this seems like confusion, the author understands the dynamic conditions involved in mission planning. The changing of targets, aircraft assignments, and the like, is just the efficient use of personnel and equipment to satisfy mission requirements.

The mission (Mx. #157) was necessary because the results from the previous mission were still unknown. The weather was bad again so an instrument approach from the west was used.

"The flak was pretty heavy and was some of the biggest they had ever shot at us. We were lucky and didn't get any holes. No fighters hit us but they were up." (JC)

Flak was often from 88-mm cannons; however, this target was on the coast at a vital harbor. Shore batteries were expected to protect the harbor from both naval and air attack. Consequently, there may have been more 105-mm cannons there than what might have been farther inland.

"Two P-51's had mid-air and fell into the drink near Tershelling Island." (RR) [Tershelling is in the Frisian Island chain off the coast of Holland.]

"The flak was moderate but again we escaped being hit." (RR) However, bomb group reports that B-17 "Sugar" (or "Sugah") from 34th's 391st BSq was heavily damaged.

In 48 hours, the 34th BGp alone had delivered 209 tons of bombs to the Kiel harbor area.

—o–o–O–o–o—

The next day, April 5 (Mx. #158), the crews were awakened at 2:30 a.m. They were to bomb an airfield at Unterschlaversbach, ten miles northwest of Nurnburg – if weather permitted visual bombing. This was going to prove a long, rough day.

They took off in weather so bad they could not assemble over England. They were to fly individually to Reims, France, and assemble there for the mission.

They climbed through bad weather for 15 minutes.

"Each minute, we were sweating out a mid-air collision." (RR)

Many hundreds of bombers were converging on the same point. The Kennedy crew in 960 B/L finally broke out of the weather at 24,000 feet.

Ten aircraft from the 34th BGp never found the formation.

One aircraft, 280 E/M from the 7th BSq (R. Martin, pilot), had to pull up steeply to avoid a mid-air collision. The bomber, encountering violent prop wash, threw the crewmen from their stations. The aircraft stalled, lowered a wing, and went into a spin. Ironically, the name of the aircraft was "Missbehaven Raven."

Most of the crew bailed out while in the spin – which was difficult to do because of the centrifugal force trying to hold the crewmen in place. The engineer, Fleming, bailed out at 20,000 feet and received broken bones in his foot. The bombardier, Leo Bartczak, bailed out but his parachute rigging fouled on the hatch door and he was strangled.

After losing nearly 12,000 feet, Martin finally regained control. He returned to the airbase with the bombardier still outside the aircraft.

The emotions of air combat and the continual risks were often of an extreme nature. And they appeared in many forms and arrived in many ways.

"Missbehaven Raven"
B-17G-85-BO 43-38280 E/M of the 7th BSq after 31
missions.

(Gary Ferrell photograph source)

The Kennedy crew aircraft assembled with the rest of the mission aircraft and continued to the target. However, clouds over the primary target necessitated going to the secondary target: Nurnburg proper.

The weather and contrails hampered vision so they flew lower in an attempt to get under the bad weather. With improved visibility, they made their bomb run and released on the target.

"Target today was Nurnburg. This sure is a rough target. Today was our third trip there and there is plenty of flak but it wasn't accurate today." (JC)

Over Nurnberg, "Dinah-Mite," 44-8284, received serious flak damage. On this aircraft was radioman Jack Share. Share's first mission had been March 10 in 960 B/L with Kennedy, Reid, Corkern and crew.

During the formation's return flight, they flew over Worms and Bad Kreznach at only 8,000 feet. The Germans in these towns used to send up a lot of flak but this time they were silent. Now these cities were occupied by Allies.

The bad weather continued and the formations descended to 2,000 feet over France. At Maastrich, Belgium, it was decided that each pilot should fly back to his airbase individually rather than risk a collision in an attempt to maintain formation.

The Corkern aircraft continued with their route over Antwerp. They were now down to 1,000 feet. "At times the soup was so thick we could not see #1 and #4 engines. That is positive – no exaggeration. We really did sweat all day but we made it back safely." (RR)

"No fighters were up. Hope they never get up." (JC)

According to 34th BGp reports, both Nurnberg and Unterschalanersbach were targeted and they received 39 tons and 48 tons of bombs, respectively. Of the 39 tons, 960 B/L contributed three.

"Dinah-Mite" did not return home; Jack Share and crewmates were down in the North Sea.

—o–o–O–o–o—

After a day off, the Kennedy crew was awakened at 1:45 a.m. for their next mission. April 7, Mx. #159, would be to an ordnance depot three miles southeast of Gustrow. This depot was supplying materiel for the war in the East. The mission would be another bad one.

They approached Gustrow just northwest of Hanover and became embroiled in an ongoing air battle with Me-262 jets, Me-109s, and FW-190s. The air battle lasted over an hour.

The Luftwaffe attacked the group ahead and behind 960 B/L. This again is perhaps a reflection of the 34th BGp's tight formations.

"I saw them shoot three B-17s out of the group ahead. One of them blew up and just made a ball of fire. At about the same time, they shot down one out of the group behind. I saw four Me-109s shot down by 'little friends'." (RR) ["Little Friends' was the affectionate name given by bomber crews to their fighter escorts.]

"Jerry fighters hit us from the battle line to the I.P., a total of 50 minutes. There were about 150 enemy fighters. I hit a Me-109 but didn't knock him down, a P-51 got him." (JC)

When they turned at their initial point to start the bomb run, Reid saw another B-17 on fire and some of the crew bail out. Seven parachutes opened. There were most likely nine crewmen onboard so perhaps the pilot and co-pilot were still with the aircraft.

"Planes were blowing up all around. I was just waiting our time but it never came." (JC)

At least the formation had the satisfaction of delivering bombs very accurately and starting many fires. The 34th BGp claimed two fighters destroyed, three probables, and four damaged.

The aircraft returned to the airbase and had to let down through thick overcast "..so we still sweated until we landed." (RR)

"The crew is still together. Lord ride with us if it is thy will." (JC)

—o–o–O–o–o—

It is possible that each time an experienced combat crewman "sweated" something, he was really displaying a level of courage the common man, the common young man does not – ever.

Flak was random and impersonal. The crew could develop a detached acceptance of simple statistics. They knew they were flying a bomber that could take abuse like none before it.

Fighter attacks were different. This was an *individual* attacking a *selected* bomber. These attacks were directed by *intelligence* not *statistics*. The bomber crews *accepted* the odds of being hit by flak – they accepted *statistics* – they *feared* the fighters; that was *personal*.

The Corkern crew mission list was growing longer and they were approaching their mission quotas. The area of occupied territory was increasing rapidly, yet the bombers were facing more determined opposition in the air.

People with no experience in combat can only wonder what these combatants' thoughts were about surviving the last missions.

A crewman flying in the Mediterranean Theatre of Operations in WWII told the author that when he started flying combat missions, he accepted that he would not return from one of them. He was a crewman in a twin-engine bomber and flew low-altitude missions. The odds just seemed too great against his survival. He was not particularly scared; he concentrated on his business in a professional manner.

However, as he was nearing the end of his combat tour, he started obsessing on the thought that he might die on one of his few remaining missions.

He flew his last three missions by forcing himself to remain calm and execute his flight tasks. In combat, he bordered on near-uncontrolled panic.

When he landed after his last mission he said there was no rejoicing. He was just too tired. He felt like a walking dead man – there was no elation. He appeared young, slim and tough, yet emotionally, inside, he was old and exhausted. This feeling lasted two months and did not fully subside for almost a year.

There are many definitions and examples of "Hero."

—o–o–O–o–o—

Chapter VII

Winding Down

The April 8 mission (Mx. #160) was over Grafenwhor with an ordnance depot and Wehrmacht barracks to be bombed – visually only.

They climbed through thick overcast and assembled at 5,000 feet.

"Flew in at 14,000 feet." (JC) This was about 6,000 feet lower than usual.

"Jerry was up again today, but didn't hit us. We were fighter bait today and destroyed around 80." (JC) [This was a humorous suggestion that the escort fighters were using the bombers to lure German fighters their direction.]

The target was hit and there was a column of smoke to nearly 12,000 feet.

There was no flak.

"Hope the luck holds out." (JC)

—o–o–O–o–o—

A B-17 from the 34th BGp's 391st BSq, 43-38972 L/C, had blown an engine cylinder. This might not have been too bad, but it was on the #4 engine. To make matters worse, the prop would not feather.

The aircraft, "Duke the Spook," piloted by Lankford, had to land at a field in France.

Merlin Bruning, his ball turret gunner, was unique in that he would connect the right clips of his parachute harness to his parachute and then twist his way into the turret with the parachute. Once seated, he would hinge the chute aside to the right and wedge it vertically against the breech of the right machine gun.

With the chute to the right, he could (with difficulty) still reach to the upper right and turn the azimuth hand crank. The chute would obstruct his view of the oxygen pressure and flow gauges, yet he felt safer with the chute.

He was sure he could clip the left side of the parachute before bailing out of the turret, or if not, then in free-fall. He also thought just one set of clips would keep the chute connected to the harness.[7]

He had never heard of another ball turret gunner taking his chute into the turret.

There were times a crewman would use a relief tube forward of the turret and the ball turret gunner's aiming window would become wet and freeze over. He would then have to position the window high and aft so someone could reach through the fuselage camera port and clean his window. This would not be a problem if the crewman told him before using the relief tube.

The "Duke the Spook" crew returned from France in a repaired B-17, but its landing gear would not retract.

It would be a month before "Duke the Spook" would be on another mission.

—o-o-O-o-o—

Now during the return flights, the crews were over more and more allied territory and the bombers could return to their airbases in East Anglia at lower altitudes.

---

[7]

It was quite likely that with only the right side hooks on the parachute, the uneven weight distribution would prevent the parachute from filling sufficiently. Still, each crewman understood his risks and tried to improve his chances however he felt he could.

Reid wrote of their return flight on this April 8 mission, "Returned over Koblenz at low level...seeing many damaged German towns and Patton's supplies   really moving in...had a clear day to land for a change. Was easy mission except for length."

It had been an eight-hour mission and they had been awake since 2:30 a.m.

—o–o–O–o–o—

"Clear day" was a much-appreciated rarity in East Anglia.

While visiting East Anglia in 1992, the author watched a video documentary about the 8th AAF in East Anglia. He was standing with a large group of 8th vets who were back for their 50th reunion.

The viewers were quiet. Each one was reminiscing with his own private memories. Then in one scene, a B-24 was shown taking off and someone asked rather loudly, "Hey, Charlie! Isn't that your outfit?"

Quietly, Charlie said, "Couldn't be...the sun's shinin'."

Few laughed.

—o–o–O–o–o—

The April 11 mission (Mx. #163) was to Treuchtlengen. The crew was still in 960 B/L and carried leaflets. This was an interesting mission because of things that did not happen.

They were awakened at 2 a.m., went to their briefings, and then flew to Treuchtlenger to bomb the railroad depot and marshaling yards. These were being used to move supplies west to resupply the Wehrmacht opposing Patton.

The target was bombed, the rails were rearranged, and then they flew back to the base.

"Target today was a marshaling yard in a small town close to Nurnburg. No flak or fighters today. It was a good mission." (JC)

Many people back in the US would think this was a "routine" mission. But a truly routine mission occurred in foul weather, with fear of mid-air collisions, with an engine running rough, while being holed by flak and attacked by fighters, and having hung-up bombs. For many crewmen, they were just trying to survive in an aircraft slowly coming apart under their feet.

This April 11 mission was *not* a "routine" mission.

—o–o–O–o–o—

Roy Reid told the author that they did not bomb Germany again because American troops were moving up so fast it was not safe to drop bombs there.

They needed three more missions to rotate home and Reid did not even keep a diary of them.

—o–o–O–o–o—

The April 14 mission (Mx. #164) was over Royan, France. The target was coastal gun emplacements and sub pens where Germans had been isolated but would not surrender. The Germans and guns were still a threat to shipping. This was an aerial "mopping up" operation.

"Target today was Royan in France on the coast. This was a milk run." (JC)

The crew was to have flown 960 B/L. It was very foggy and the British had been working on the hard stands and there were some holes nearby. These holes were marked with clearance lights, but Kennedy did not turn 960 B/L properly and a wheel dropped into a hole, causing a prop to be damaged when it struck the ground.

The clever engineer, Cleo Baughman, jumped from the aircraft and extinguished all the clearance lights marking the holes. This way, they could claim that the holes were not properly illuminated and the aircraft damage was not their fault.

Then the crew moved to aircraft 44-6938 and continued with the mission.

Baughman was a very resourceful engineer. It had been he who opened the camera hatch to push on the ball turret door so Corkern could rotate the turret and have the door properly secured.

Cleo Baughman *(Corkern photograph source.)*

April 15 (Mx. #165) was another mission over Royan, France. This time they were back in 960 B/L.

"It was a milk run again. The French took it right after we bombed. The coast is really tore up." (JC)

Besides Corkern's completing his next-to-last mission on April 15, he received a Good Conduct Medal that day.

Corkern, Reid, Kennedy, and most of the crew, needed one more mission, and on April 16, they completed their tour of duty with another mission (Mx. #166) to the Royan area – in 960 B/L. Target was German coastal guns.

"Target today was Granepoint, France. It was a milk run. No fighters. No nothing. I sure was glad too. This does it for us. The End." (JC) [There are double underlines under "The End" in Corkern's mission log.]

—o–o–O–o–o—

Their co-pilot, "Scotty" O'Brien, needed a few more missions to rotate home so he was assigned to pilot Elmer Rawson's crew. On June 28, O'Brien was co-pilot to Rawson on the "No Gum Chum" flight back to the US. The aircraft had flown 74 missions.

—o–o–O–o–o—

Navigator Roy Reid returned to the US and went to Ellington Army Air Base in Texas to train as a B-29 navigator in the Pacific. However, the war ended and he was discharged in Arkansas, October 1945.

He returned to college and completed his last semester.

He and Sybil (Holloway) had two daughters, Janet Knowles and Karen Buss.

"Shorty" Corkern, with his Air Medal and four Oak Leafs, returned to the US and received his discharge on October 25, 1945; exiting at Keesler Army Air Force Base, Biloxi, Mississippi.

His military separation documents state that his Related Civilian Occupation was *"Airplane armorer/gunner -- Flew 33 missions over Germany and occupied territory with 8th AAF. Installed guns before flight and fired ball turret guns under combat conditions."*

The need for such experience in civilian life can be questioned.

James U. and Gilberta Ruth Corkern

(Corkern photograph source)

James U. Corkern had two sons, James Urban, Jr. and Dennis Keith, and a daughter, Sharon Ruth.

He passed away May 4, 1987.

His son, James Jr., was a C-130 pilot in Vietnam.

His grandson, (James Jr.'s son) Major Gregory Bryan Corkern, was a helicopter pilot with two tours of duty in Iraq; three generations serving their nation aloft.

James Corkern Sr's, wife, Gilberta Ruth (Armstrong) Corkern is, no doubt, very proud of her family.

"The Straggler"

by T/Sgt. Orvil Lindsey

I saw a Fort knocked out of its group,
Afire and in despair.
With the Nazi fighters surrounding her,
As it flew alone back there.

The Messerschmitts came barreling through,
Throwing a hail of lead
At the crippled Fort that wouldn't quit,
Though two of its engines were dead.

But a couple of props kept straining away,
And here, guns were blazing too
As she stayed in the air in that Hell back there,
And fought like the Fortresses do.

Four times a fighter belched fire and smoke,
Four times a fighter went down,
As the Fortress kept winging home,
And the nerve of the crew stayed sound.

But time after time the fighters came back,
And attacked the lagging plane.
I knew she couldn't last for long,
And my heart was touched with pain.

Her gunners fought a bitter fight,
But now the guns were still.
And a fighter, seeing the time was ripe
Came in to make the kill.

A stream of lead ripped into a tank,
And the Fort exploded in two,
And somewhere the angels prepared a place
For a weary Fortress crew.

From *Mendlesham Memories*, Sept. 2001

Afterword

Corkern may have completed his tour of duty but the aircraft, B-17G-75- BO-43-37960, had not completed its tour.

Between April 18 and 19, the aircraft flew its last three bombing missions in the 34th BGp's 18th BSq. These were flown with three different crews flying missions 168, 169, and 170, to Kolin, Aussig, and Nauen, respectively.

—o–o–O–o–o—

April 30, 1945, Adolph Hitler committed suicide.

—o–o–O–o–o—

From May 1 to May 7, B-17G 960 B/L flew different kinds of missions. It was not carrying bombs or leaflets; with four different aircrews, it made four food deliveries in Operation Chowhound. These were mercy flights to feed the starving Dutch.

May 8, the day after 960 B/L's last Operation Chowhound mission, the war in Europe ended. But 960 B/L had one more mission in Europe.

On May 15, 960 B/L assisted in the ferrying of just-released POWs and displaced persons from recently liberated territory. There were likely several such ferry flights.

—o–o–O–o–o—

June 21, 960 B/L returned to the US, landing at Bradley Field, New Hampshire. On these return flights the B-17 carried eleven passengers besides the nine-man crew.

The next day, 960 B/L was flown to a converging depot at South Plains Army Airfield, Lubbock, Texas.

The following winter, December 19, 1945, B-17G 43-37960 aka "960 B/L" was ferried to Kingman, Arizona – to await scrapping.

Those who can afford the emotional attachment to a machine can justifiably feel saddened by 960 B/L's departure. And they can be in awe with the thought, 'Wouldn't it be great if 960 B/L could have been preserved and displayed somewhere...or better, it could have been maintained on flight status!'

All understand why this was not likely.

But understanding does not really matter.

It is acceptable to feel the loss of the Machine.

And the Warrior Heros can still be missed.

— End —

Appendix - A

THE MACHINE

BOEING B-17G FLYING FORTRESS

The Flying Fortress of interest is B-17G-75-BO (s/n 43-37960) 960 B/L. Details of that particular aircraft are limited; however, its lineage is clear.

The Boeing B-17 went through many modifications, and each major modification produced a different model number. The greater the change, the more the number was changed.

Thus the last fighting B-17s were the B-17E, then B-17F, and finally B-17G.

There were changes within these configurations such as B-17G-73, -74, -75, etc., and there were even changes within each of these. There was also a code to indicate which company manufactured it.

Five more modifications after the B-17G-75 configuration produced the -80; the last combat model, or close to it.

All B-17s had similar shapes but it was the "E" that first had the familiar profile that is thought of when "B-17" is heard or read.

The easiest way to identify the "E" is by the nose. It had multi-paneled sections of Plexiglas with an optically-flat panel of glass in the lower front section. This glass panel permitted the bombardier to have an undistorted view through the bombsight.

Some B-17s had a limited-movement, remotely-controlled Bendix top turret, with the gunner aiming through a small Plexiglas dome. The first 113 B-17E's had a similar arrangement for a Bendix belly turret, but this was unsatisfactory and the Sperry ball turret was installed. It was standard on all subsequent models with lower guns.

There were 512 "E"s manufactured.

The "F" had a frameless, one-piece, fully-blown Plexiglas nose, but like all others had the flat glass section for the bombardier. In an effort to protect it against frontal attacks by fighters, a single .50 caliber gun mount was provided in protrusions on each side of the nose. These permitted forward protection and were known as "cheek" guns.

A less obvious change was the increased width of the prop blades. The engine cowlings had to be redesigned so these wider blades would clear the cowling when they were fully feathered. These cowlings had a greater forward radius than that on the Model "E."

The increased "bite" of these props improved many operational specifications. All in all, to produce an "F" rather than an "E", over 400 changes were needed; some minor, some major.

There were selected modifications made at field centers after the aircraft left the factory. Navigation-sighting Plexiglas domes might be added to one series, a single .50 caliber gun mounted in the Plexiglas nose of another series, etc.

One waist gunner sometimes interfered with the movement of the other, so these gun ports were enlarged and staggered...the right gun station being about three feet forward of the left. This was not a minor modification. All the skin and formers up to ten feet aft from the right wing trailing edge had to be changed.

Boeing designed and manufactured the B-17, but as with many aircraft in WWII, their need required that other factories construct them as well. Of the total 3,405 "F"s built, Boeing built 2,300 at their Seattle, Washington plant; Lockheed built 500 in their Vega, California, plant; and Douglas built 605 at their Long Beach, California, plant. The letter identifiers in the aircraft serial numbers have "BO" for those built by Boeing; "VE" for those built by Lockheed; and "DL" for those built by Douglas.

As quickly as the B-17Fs were built, they were rushed to Europe to replace the battle-scarred B-17Es. These B-17E aircrews had suffered many losses early on while the 8th AAF was learning how to make war.[8]

The "G" first flew May 21, 1943, and the first production model was delivered September 4, 1943. The "G"s were built in the greatest number with Boeing building 4,035; Lockheed/Vega, 2,250; and Douglas, 2,395; for a total of 8,680 planes. The cost for a B-17G was near $190,000 in 1940 dollars. (In 2005 dollars, this would be approximately $2.5 million each.)

The "G" had the same nose glazing as the "F" but it had a remotely controlled Bendix chin turret. These were on all subsequent B-17s. This turret is the distinctive feature of the "G," yet the last 86 "F"s also had this turret. (Plane spotters take notice – B-17F-75 had chin turrets.)

The top turret of the "G" had a different shape from those on previous models. The first "G" did not have the cheek gun placements, but subsequent aircraft did.

—o-o-O-o-o—

<hr>

[8] The first B-17 and aircrew to complete 25 missions was the Memphis Belle; a B-17F. The bomber was brought home to help sell War Bonds. Generally, only the aircrew rotated home and the bomber lumbered on in combat with a new aircrew. The B-17s were flown until shot down, excessively damaged, or simply worn out.

The staggered waist gun positions now had gun ports through completely enclosed Plexiglas windows (finally). In the combat area, the "E"s and "F"s simply had large, open ports.

The tail gun station was modified at the United Air Lines Modification Center in Cheyenne, Wyoming. This was called the "Cheyenne" tail turret. It provided the tail gunner increased visibility, the guns traversed a greater arc than guns mounted on the previous models' gimbals, and the gunner aimed by a reflector gunsight rather than the old mechanical ring-and-bead sight. The United Air Lines Modification Center updated 5,534 B-17s between 1942 and 1945.

Previous B-17s might have had several color schemes. In some cases, it was the prerogative of the airbase commander to camouflage the top wing surfaces. However, the Vega-built B-17G-25s were the first to be delivered in a natural aluminum finish with black letters and numbers. This made the aircraft more visible, yet strangely, there was no increase in combat losses. Producing aircraft in natural aluminum saved much time, and weight was saved by not using zinc chromate primer and an over-paint.

The maximum weight of the "G" was 12,250 pounds heavier than the previous "F" models, yet with the same bomb load it could fly farther.

Eighty-five B-17Gs were delivered to the Royal Air Force (RAF) and some of these subsequently received H2S BTO (Bombing Through Overcast) radar systems, called "Mickey Radar." These were mounted in large chin bubbles. The RAF was first to utilize radar in aerial combat and this radar system was later modified to fit in a ball configuration and mounted in some US B-17Gs.

These "leader" aircraft were used when overcast obscured ground targets, and in Western Europe, this was often. In flight, they were easily recognized by their "deeper ball turrets."

Captured B-17Gs were used by the Luftwaffe for dropping supplies and spies, for reconnaissance, and training Luftwaffe fighter pilots on attack procedures.

Some of the B-17G's workhorse legend comes from "shuttle missions" where a flight of B-17s took off in England and flew to Russia, then flew to Africa, and finally flew back to England...bombing a different target on each leg of the triangle.

B-17G Specifications

Span	103' 9.4"
Length	74' 3.9" (with Cheyenne tail)
Height	19' 2.4"
Power	4 x Wright R-1820-97 Cyclone, 1,000 hp @ 2300 rpm @ 25,000'
Empty Weight	36,134 lbs.
Gross Weight	40,260 lbs.
Cruising Speed	160 mph
Top Speed	302 mph
Ceiling	36,400'
Range	3,750 miles
Aircrew	10 (or 9 in combat)
Bomb Load	6 x 1600 lbs. and 2 x 4000 lbs.
Armament	11 x .50 caliber machine guns (up to 13 x .50 cal.)

Please note: All tables of all aircraft figures are incorrect...when considering all options. The B-17G could carry 17,600 pounds of bombs, but only a short distance. Normally, 6,000 pounds is quoted; however, the volume of the bomb bay might limit the weight because of bomb size, i.e. 2 ea. 2,000 pound bombs, or 2 ea. 1,600 pound; or 2 ea. 1,000; 12 ea. 500s; 16 ea. 300s;16 ea. 250; 20 ea. 100; etc.

Additionally – Range is often given as the maximum distance flown; or it could be assumed to be the radius of that distance. The B-17G could nominally fly 3,750 miles; this means it could reach a target 1,875 miles from its base and return...depending on bomb load.

With a fuel capacity of 1,700 gallons and carrying 17,600 pounds of bombs, the range was 3,400 miles.

The last "G" was produced at the Vega, California plant on July 29, 1945.

Workhorse, indeed.

Appendix - B

THE ORGANIZATION

THE 34TH BOMB GROUP

The 34th BGp was activated at Langley Field, Virginia on January 15, 1941, nearly a year before the US entered the war. This makes them one of the oldest bomb groups of WWII.

The unit later incorporated the 1st Reconnaissance Squadron as one of the 34th BGp squadrons. That squadron's long-range missions along the coasts and out to sea provided an experience-base for the general purpose of the 34th.

The 34th was moved first to Walla Walla, Washington, and then to the hottest place in the US: Blythe, California.

Ground crewmen remember that any metal aircraft in the sun became a large aluminum heat sink and even standing on the wings burned their feet – through their military boots. When around the aircraft, shirt sleeves were rolled down in case a sweaty arm touched the aircraft's hot surface. Heavy maintenance was often performed at night. Sand storms made precision work difficult.

There was so little air-conditioning on the base that personnel were permitted to sleep in the base theater...on unpadded, twelve-inch-wide benches.

At Blythe, the 34th became a training school for crews identified for combat duty. The training was in B-17s but the group later converted to B-24s. Some of the first bomber crews in the Pacific and Atlantic were trained by the 34th at Blythe.

The 34th, at that time, was not a designated combat unit but this changed January 5, 1944, when the 34th was identified as a 2nd AAF operational unit. The last day of March that year, they started moving to a Midwestern field for overseas processing, and from there to West Palm Beach, Florida, where they would depart the US for a theater of war.

On April 9, 1944, the first flights left Florida flying south toward the West Indies. One hour into the flight, a sealed envelope was opened and they learned their destination was England.

The first flight landed at Valley Aerodrome in Britain on April 17, after flying from Florida to Natal, Brazil; then east to Dakar, Africa; from there north to Marrakesh, French Morocco; and then north to Britain.

On April 18, 1944, the first 34th BGp B-24s started landing at recently-constructed Station 156 adjacent to the little village of Mendlesham, Suffolk County, England, a region known generally as East Anglia.

Unfortunately, aircrews, staff, and ground personnel started arriving more quickly than beds, blankets, and black-out curtains.

The night of their arrival, the airbase was bombed. Perhaps, "bombed at" would be more accurate since only a half-dozen bombs fell within a mile of the runways.

However, the sky was lit with search lights, and there was the flash and noise of bombs. Overhead were the sounds of engines, including Merlins from British aircraft attacking the German bombers. No German bombers were seen, but the unique sounds of their engines would not be forgotten.

This informed 34th personnel that they had entered a war zone – had there been doubts before. Seventy-two 34th BGp bombers would be flying from the US and landing at Mendlesham, and there would eventually be nearly 3,000 men stationed there.

Almost immediately upon their arrival, they began intense practice missions with simulated bombing runs and dummy bombs. Flight crews spent many hours practicing aircraft formation assembly and rallying operations, as well as formation flying. This was in addition to the several hundred hours of formation flying already logged in California. Their ability to hold tight formations contributed to their survival during Luftwaffe attacks.

The 34th flight crews had many courses and lectures by both American and RAF combat veterans.

The crews were awakened at dawn on several mornings in succession and they wondered as they went through their mission preparations if this was to be their first mission or just another simulation. May 23, 1944, was Mission #1 – a bombing raid on Etampes Mondesir, France.

The 34th BGp had four squadrons; 4th, 7th, 18th, and 391st. They flew sixty-three missions with B-24s, then started transitioning to B-17s. Their first B-17 mission was September 17, 1944.

Also in September, the 4th BSq was reorganized as the center of a Pathfinder Squadron. These aircraft were to support the entire 93rd Bomb Wing, so besides the 34th BGp, they also led the 485 BGp, 490 BGp, and 493 BGp. This makes it difficult to determine details of the 4th BSq's missions.

The mission assembly area for the 34th BGp was a 3 x 12-mile rectangle extending southeast from a beacon near Malden, 40 miles south-southwest of Mendlesham. Malden is on the River Blackwater, which exits into the wide Blackwater estuary. This made it easy to locate in good weather – which did not occur often in East Anglia.

The southeast corner of the assembly area was over the Channel.

Air Traffic For One Day [9]

As a land area, Britain (94,217 sq. mi.) is about the same size as the state of Michigan. And no place in Britain is farther than 75 miles from a coastline.

Imagine packing into this Michigan-sized area nearly 700 airfields and landing strips. This was the condition during WWII.

By necessity, airfields were so close that one airfield's traffic pattern overlapped another's, thus making air traffic control a serious problem. It was made even worse in bad weather – which was often the case.

Most airfields were constructed on a common design with one 6,000-foot runway intersected by two 5,200-foot runways, making an equilateral triangle.

The runways' general alignment was similar because of the prevailing winds and flat terrain; consequently, recognizing one's home airbase was difficult and getting lost was easy.

There were few large cities, few railway tracks, the towns looked similar, the little villages were numerous, and the countryside was laced with stone borders in myriad shapes and sizes. With the different colors of the fields changing seasonally, the ground simply looked like WWI "dazzle camouflage."

There were few major rivers, and in East Anglia, because of the flat terrain and low elevation, there were miles of wandering, twisting drainage basins which changed shape and size depending on tide and wind.

---

[9]

Much of this is from public domain but there were confusing comments and it was therefore considerably amended by the author.

Early on, for security reasons, there was a minimum of radio communication. Air traffic control relied on clever formal (and many informal) methods of routing the aircraft to the correct airbases.

The AAF, specializing in daytime operations, might launch a mission involving 2,500+ four-engine bombers with some 1,200 fighter escorts. The RAF, engaged in night bombing, might have a similar number aloft during the same 24 hours. This went on for weeks at a time.

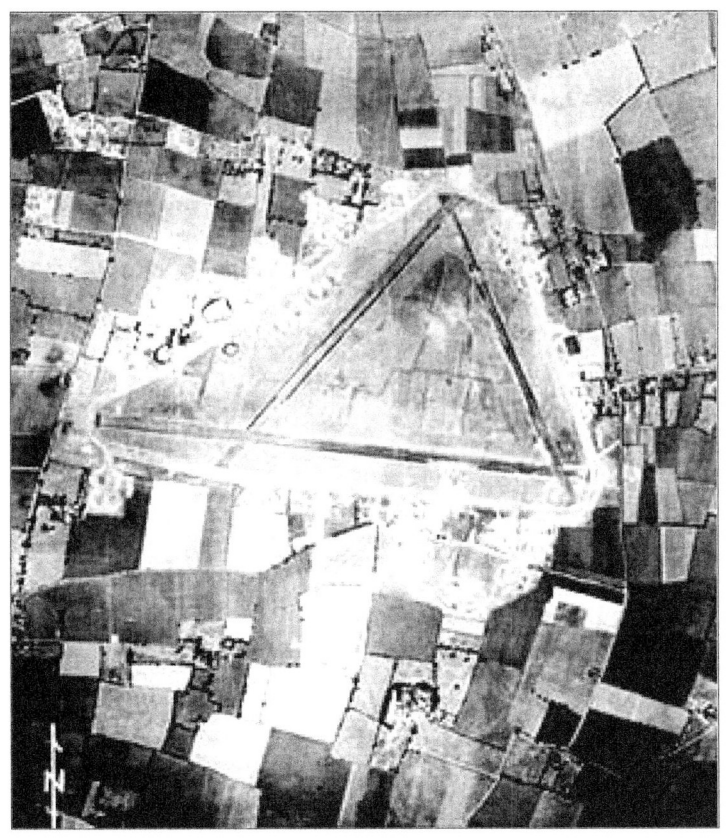

Station 156, Mendlesham

(Paul Gustafson photograph source)

There were several electronic navigation systems used by the 34th BGp. These earlier units were referred to as "radar" but they were of the most elementary type.

The weather, always a factor, became less of an obstacle for bombing when the lead aircraft had radar. There were large radomes mounted where a ball turret would customarily have been.

Early systems used transmissions from ground-based antennas and the navigator could interpret these on a screen to determine the aircraft's position.

Subsequent systems had similar electronic information coupled directly to the bombsight; this information permitted much more accurate zero-visibility bombing. This was more like modern radar with transmitting and receiving equipment in the aircraft and providing ground images on a screen.

"Blind bombing" was first used in October 1944.

In November 1944, only two months after the better imaging systems became available, seven of ten missions were "blind" missions and the accuracy of two of the seven were rated as "good" by post-mission photo interpretation. By January 1945, the majority of missions were by instruments.

Instrument bombing raids contributed significantly to the overall war effort, particularly considering the generally bad weather over western Europe.

Though these imaging radar systems replaced the ball turret on the lead aircraft, when the high-flying bombers were executing their missions, they were over thick, closed-in weather and often the Luftwaffe was grounded. This radar permitted bombing raids in any weather, increasing the opportunity for damage on the ground, while reducing the opportunity for the Luftwaffe to intercept the bombers.

The title "bombardier" was used less and the term "toggler" used. This was a crewman who "toggled" the bomb release in his aircraft on cue from the lead aircraft.

A chronological list of 34th BGp targets shows an advancing line from just outside of Paris to the most distant border of Germany. As the Allied ground forces advanced faster and occupied more territory, the number of bombing targets decreased – they were simply running out of targets.

The 34th BGp's last wartime mission, Mx. #170, was on April 20, 1945. They had flown 170 missions and had lost 34 aircraft.

—o–o–O–o–o—

Then the 34th turned their bombers into aerial freighters, dropping food to the Dutch.

VE-Day was anticipated and eagerly awaited – finally, on May 8, 1945, it arrived and the expected parties began.

Bright fire and smoke had become such a part of their lives, it was natural that there would be an outbreak of spontaneous firing of ferry pistols launching the familiar colored flares.

Then the 34th BGp converted from hauling freight to hauling passengers, and in this case, they were part of a large aerial fleet flying just-released prisoners and displaced persons out of Austria. Each B-17 carried 30 passengers (one carried 31), and in such emergency conditions, a reduced crew of four or five. This helped the aircrews unwind doing something familiar and useful.

Mendlesham's Station 156 started to see its ranks decrease as personnel were sent home.

On June 19, the first flight element of the air group took off, but instead of heading east, this time they were heading west...to the US. A major westward air corridor was established and the 8th AAF did what it could to fill it.

The 34th BGp alone returned 72 of their squadron's B-17s to the US. Some of these were old "war wearies" like "Betty" with 71 missions. Piloting one B-17 home was Raymond Myers, who had been MIA after being forced down behind Russian lines.

By early August, Mendlesham had been released from the noise and business of making war. The four-engine bombers were no longer taking off 40 at a time, flying low over village and farm, and they were no longer returning, some smoking, some with obvious battle damage.

The little village of Mendlesham, a village whose history started somewhere in the distant past before people kept records, was left with memories of young American airmen who had walked their few streets and enjoyed their pubs and hospitality.

Mendlesham was quiet again. And so was the 34th Bomb Group. Its four squadrons – 4th, 7th, 18th, and 391st – were deactivated by September 2, 1945.

Appendix - C

MENDLESHAM, SUFFOLK, ENGLAND
(East Anglia)

Mendlesham, a small village in Suffolk County, is very old...no one knows how old.

In the 400s, as more Angles from the Jutland peninsula (Denmark), raided this low area of England, they displaced the Romano-British who had been living there as Romanized Celts for 400 years.

The Angles were not the only raiders to come to England during this time. They were a part of an overall, unorganized invasion by near-relatives: Saxons, Jutes, and Frisians – all Northwestern Europeans.

The Angles shared their name to identify East Anglia and "Suffolk," which translates from "southern folk." This distinguished them from "northern folk" – "Norfolk." The Angles gave their name to their Germanic language.

There is but a small, semantic step from the Angles speaking "Anglesch" to their speaking "Englesch" – and "English."

The village was known as "Mendlesham" well before the 1090s when the Domesday Book was compiled. This was a survey and inventory prepared by the warring (yet orderly) Norman French. The Normans had started forcing their rule and culture on England in 1066. The Normans had originally come from the same basic people as the Angles. "Normans" had been "Northmen" or "Norse" – a Germanic people.

In the Domesday Book, it is written...

"Mendlesham   Mele(s)ham/Melnesham/-ssam   /Menlessam/ Mud(d)lesham: King's land, kept by Godric. Church. Large; moated site."

This was written in a Norman clerical (Latin) shorthand. The entry meant that "Mendlesham" was the modern name (for 1087) but on earlier kings' tax roles, it was "Melesham," and on some roles was "Melnesam," and other variants.

The purpose of the Domesday Book was to update ancient tax surveys for the benefit of the new Norman overlords. In some Domesday entries, even quarts of honey were inventoried for tax purposes.

Mendlesham belonged to whomever was king. In 1087, someone named Godric (not a Norman name) was the tenant-in-chief. There was a church and a structure with a moat. This, a king would be interested in knowing.

King William likely gave a Norman baron a fiefdom that enclosed Mendlesham village.

—o–o–O–o–o—

In April 1944, Mendlesham was within walking distance of some of the outlying living quarters of Mendlesham airbase, known also as Station 156.

Mendlesham had three pubs: the "Fleece," "King's Head," and "Magpie."

The "Fleece" is still there; the name recognizes the importance of wool to the British post-plague (1349) economy. The "King's Head," also still there, is a reference to King Charles I – who lost his.

The Kennedy/Corkern B-17 crew navigator was Roy Reid, and long after the war, Reid's daughter, Janet Reid Knowles, and husband, visited Mendlesham and lunched at the "Fleece" and then walked over to the "King's Head." Local people remembered "those brave lads" from back then.

Both pubs have bomber crew photos on the walls commemorating the days of the nearby 34th BGp. Janet Knowles was surprised to see a photo of the Kennedy crew, including her father and James Corkern on the wall of the "King's Head."[10]

Roy, who has not been back, thinks flight engineer Cleo Baughman or pilot Grant Kennedy gave the photograph to the pub during a post-war visit.

Where the base was located, there is now a TV transmitter, some light industry, and agricultural fields. And at the now-unused base runway, there is large stone monument commemorating the sacrifices of the personnel of the 34th BGp.

The ladies of Mendlesham, who maintain the grounds around the stone, placed flowers there on September 11, 2001.

Mendlesham is still a small village but it has a large heart.

Unlike many of America's allies from those years, they remember.

—o–o–O–o–o—

---

[10] In April, 2003, Janet flew in the Collings Foundation B-17G. She sat in the navigator's seat where her father had spent so many hours.

Plaque on monument at Station 156, Mendlesham.

Presentation of photograph by Cliff Hall (left), Secretary of Friends of the Eighth, and Bill Fulton, 34th BGp, 4th BSq, to Fleece landlord John Rowe (right). October 12, 1984.

(Harold Province photograph source)

Appendix - D

LUFTWAFFE TACTICS IN APRIL 1945

Before America entered WWII, the RAF bomber command had learned that no matter how tight their bomber formations flew, no matter how well the bombers were armed, or how brave their aircrews, the bomber was no match for a determined, accomplished, and equally brave Luftwaffe fighter pilot...and early in the war the German pilot had more combat experience and better equipment.

In 1942, when the US 8th AAF arrived in Britain to start precision daylight bombing, they, too, thought a tightly-flown bomber squadron could provide adequate, mutual protection. They were relying on the overlapping fields-of-fire from the bombers' machine guns. This, they thought, would discourage the Luftwaffe fighters...at least to the point that bomber losses would be acceptable for the amount of damage the bombers caused.

Just a couple of missions demonstrated that this was patently untrue. Most memorable was the October 14, 1943, raid on the ball-bearing plant at Schweinfurt in the heart of Germany. Of the 291 B-17s making the raid, 60 were shot down (540-600 crewmen lost) and 138 B-17s badly damaged.

It was only when the longer-ranged escort fighters such as the P-51 entered service that bomber losses started to lessen to an acceptable level.

So the point was made early that the Luftwaffe pilots were very good and even some of the newer, less-experienced pilots flying well-balanced aircraft could inflict considerable damage on a bomber formation – providing the Luftwaffe fighters were not intercepted by American fighters.

Germany's most successful fighter pilot was Erich Hartmann who shot down an astounding 352 aircraft. Though his combat was over the Eastern Front, there were German aces on the Western Front who specialized in shooting down bombers.

Herbert Rollwage shot down 44 four-engine bombers. Considering the damage such a bomber could inflict on German citizens and materiel, and that each of these bombers generally had nine crewmen, Rollwage made quite a contribution to the defense of his country.

Walther Dahl shot down 36 four-engine bombers. Two other German aces, Werner Schroer and Hugo Frey, shot down 26 each; the next, Egon Mayer, 25; then the next, 24; then 21, etc. These six Luftwaffe pilots shot down over 200 four-engine bombers; 1,800 crewmen.

When weather permitted, Germany continued to put up formidable fighters against the bombers. The Me-109G(-10) was a superb fighter but had been outclassed by the American P-47 and P-51. However, even with these, the outcome of fighter combat was far from certain when they faced each other one-on-one.

The FW-190D, a more recent fighter than the Me-109 series, was always a dangerous aircraft, particularly against bombers.

German fighter production remained high even in the latter days of the war. The Luftwaffe was simply running out of fuel. New pilots arrived for combat with minimum flight time because of the shortage of fuel for training.

All Luftwaffe fighter configurations culminated in the introduction of the Me-262. This was a twin-jet fighter with sufficient fuel and firepower to quickly blow large pieces off any bomber. Jet fuel was never as scarce as fuel for reciprocating engines.

Besides cannon, it often carried 12 individually fired, 55-mm (2-inch diameter) air-to-air rockets.

Initially, there were two active squadrons of Me-262s; the first becoming operational early October 1944. They shot down their first B-17 that month.

The Luftwaffe was shooting down more bombers than the flak and something had to be done about them. The bombers had all the protection that could be devised and it still was not enough.

—o–o–O–o–o—

It is understood that a direct attack on another nation's ability to wage aerial warfare is of paramount importance. Studies conducted between WWI and WWII indicate it; before WWII, the German Condor Legion demonstrated it in the Spanish civil war, and the Luftwaffe demonstrated it against Poland. The Battle of Britain convinced everyone.

In the Battle of Britain, RAF airfields were being bombed and the battle was going in favor of the Luftwaffe. The British thought their aerial defense of Britain might be counted in just a few weeks. Then the Luftwaffe shifted their attacks from airfields to cities. This German decision permitted Britain to survive.

Attacking the aircrew is the thinking in a tactical war. The thinking in a strategic war is that the many airbases can be attacked, or attacks can be directed against a few critical resources – like ball bearings and oil refineries, or the marshaling yards through which this materiel passed.

The actual concentrated attacks on Luftwaffe fighters began March 21, 1945. During this time, the distance between the Western and Eastern Fronts had become so short that the Luftwaffe could combine all defensive aircraft when necessary, providing fuel was available.

Luftwaffe fighters intercepting bomber formations had a difficult time. Regardless of escorts, a fighter flying through the tight boxes of B-17 formations was exposed to a lot of guns.

Each bomber might have as many as ten gun stations with a total of fourteen .50 caliber machine guns. Bombers could start firing when the fighter was 800 yards away; for the German 30-mm cannons to be effective, the fighter needed to be within 250 yards.

The 2-inch-diameter rockets had a range of 650 yards – and the twelve could be fired as a salvo. With the spreading of the rockets, they covered a large area.

The fighters preferred to attack bombers at the edges of the formations, or better yet, attack stragglers that had received flak damage and were struggling to get home on three engines.

In aerial combat, with many aircraft in the sky, a fighter pilot attacking a bomber could concentrate so intensely on hitting his target, he might develop tunnel vision. When he decided to break off the attack, he may have approached too closely to avoid a collision.

There were cases when a fighter pilot in a turn to attack one bomber, would so miscalculate his turn, that while avoiding one bomber, he would collide with another.

On many occasions the sky was filled with aircraft and collisions were a fact of the mission, not only in bad weather but in any combat.

But something happened in early April 1945 that would cause even a casual student of aerial warfare to wonder why the number of collisions increased so dramatically.

—o-o-O-o-o—

April 7, 1945, a large formation of B-17s and B-24s were en route to bomb an aircraft factory at Gustrow, Germany.

At least 60 Luftwaffe fighters broke through the escorts' defenses while the escorts were busy with other German fighters. The Me-109s and FW-190s attacked the formations for nearly forty-five minutes. The German pilots were closer to home and could use more of their fuel for combat.

Fighters collided with two bombers from the 452nd BGp and then one from the 388th BGp. Then one from the 385th BGp.

An Me-109 collided with a B-17 from the 490th BGp and the fighter pilot was killed – but the B-17 kept flying.

A fighter collided with a lead B-24 from 389th BGp and that bomber collided with the backup lead aircraft and both went down.

A fighter collided with a B-24 from the 467th BGp. The B-24's right fin and rudder was torn away. Fortunately, the twin-tail bomber flew far enough for its crew to bail out over Allied territory.

Some collisions were considered to be the result of over-zealous, inexperienced German pilots. Certainly they had many young pilots who arrived in combat with insufficient training, but there is another explanation that is accepted now as fact.

This could be nothing other than a deliberate plan to crash Luftwaffe fighters into bombers.

This does not match what was known of the Luftwaffe. This seems comparable to the Kamikaze-thinking in the Pacific.

Of 18 bombers missing after the battle, 8 fell from the sky because they were rammed.

Sixty Luftwaffe fighters had come through the escort defense. There were about 12 jets, and initially, these provided top-cover protection for Me-109s and FW-190s to break into the formations.

—o-o-O-o-o—

Several factors are involved in ramming. First is that the thought of running out of fuel is not as important, not when the ramming aircraft was not going back to its base.

And when the fighter pilot intends to ram a bomber, he has to get some hits on the bomber with his machine guns and cannons as he continues his approach. But if he is going to ram the bomber, why fire at all?

However, an aircraft prepared to ram a bomber will also receive a lot of hits from the bomber's gunners before it can get close enough to ram it.

William F. Creek, B-17 gunner with the 34th BGp, wrote of how he shot down an Me-109 that day and he has vivid memories of the plane's attack. He could see he was getting hits on the aircraft but the pilot made no effort to alter his course. It kept approaching, but then it started smoking and passed near Creek's bomber.

He could clearly see the pilot's head leaning on the right side of the Me-109's canopy.

Yet, in this close pass, the Me-109 pilot never fired his machine guns or cannons. Perhaps his guns were not charged, or they were jammed, or he could have been out of ammunition, yet it was early in the fighter attack and the aircraft had both machine guns and cannons. It would have been strange if both independent gun systems had become inoperative.

There were people who routinely monitored German aircraft radio frequencies. On this mission, they heard German martial and patriotic music, and occasionally, a woman's voice telling the pilots of their duty to the Fatherland, of mothers suffering under American bombs, or wives and sweethearts wanting to live in a free Germany. It was inspirational radio.

Jane's publications, an authoritative source, have stated that suicidal ramming was the expressed plan and purpose of some of the Luftwaffe fighters.

Roger Freeman wrote in detail that "Ramstaffel" (the Ramming Squadron) existed as such.

There were many German pilots in Sonderkommando Elbe. This was a new squadron of volunteers for an undisclosed "special" assignment. The invitation to volunteer had come from the head of the Luftwaffe, Goring himself.

Of the nearly 300 volunteers, only about half met the selection criteria. Perhaps the most predominant desired characteristics were dedication, the loss of relatives from bombing, and their susceptibility to propaganda tailored for the "special" assignment.

As explained, it was not to be a "suicide" mission but one of approaching a bomber, "aiming at a point of the fuselage between wing and tail and when collision was assured, bailing out." It does not seem that the time between being assured of collision and bailing out was a sufficient period.

From the beginning, these young men were indoctrinated to their task as were the Kamikaze pilots. They received predominately political training.[11]

At the time of the "Ramstaffel," every German combat officer knew what the final outcome of the war would be. The Russians were pressing the outskirts of Berlin. Indeed, in just two weeks, Adolph Hitler would commit suicide.

---

[11] The 'Last Hurrah' for the Luftwaffe had actually occurred shortly after the first of the year with Operation Big Blow. It was a blow-out...for American fighter planes. American losses were replaced in two weeks; the Luftwaffe losses could not be made up. And the likelihood of this result was known by the German officers who had planned the operation.

The major cities of Germany were so damaged that there was intermittent electricity, open water mains, interrupted gas lines, and public transit hardly crawled through rubble-filled streets.

Only a month before this suicide attack, over a two-week period, Dresden had been bombed by 1,600 bombers; during this same time, Berlin received bombs from 1,000 bombers – on one raid.

Bombers formed "streets" that stretched as far as one could see...one "street" going east, a return "street" going back west.

Day after day, almost any bomber that could wage war was sent on a bombing mission. Indeed, one bomber crew in the 303rd BGp, 427th BSq, had six of its nine members complete their required thirty missions in only fifty-seven days! Though it is sure that it seemed longer to them.

For comparison – still flying combat late in the war were a few Luftwaffe fighter pilots who had experienced combat in the Battle of Britain and had even flown on the first day of the invasion of Poland. They did not rotate home.

So why the suicide attack?

Propaganda.

It was at work even this late in the war. It was to continue the Hitler Myth, the belief in the near-messianic aura of a great warrior hero who would lead his nation from poverty and disgrace into a Utopian Germanic World.

In retrospect, nothing as grand as that was expected by the people.

The aerial suicide attacks can simply be explained as the desperate 'fight and die' mentality which had permeated the ground war and later submarine warfare; it had finally reached the skies.

—o-o-O-o-o—

Appendix - E

"DINAH-MITE"

Near 2 a.m., April 5, 1945, the flight crew of B-17G "Dinah-Mite" (44-8284) was awakened to start their day as an assigned bomber crew of the 8th AAF, 93rd Bomb Wing, 34th BGp, 18th BSq. They were stationed at Mendlesham, Suffolk County, East Anglia, Great Britain.

The aircrew consisted of George Mehling, pilot; Wendell Huntley, co-pilot; Harrison Britton, navigator; Robert Lampey, ball turret gunner; Lucius (Lou) Morgan, tail gunner; Stephan Niatas, flight engineer/top turret gunner; Albert Deines, waist gunner; Russell Harris, bombardier; and Jack Share, radioman.[12]

The crew went through their morning rituals, including breakfast and a visit to the chapel en route to the mission briefing. The weather was terrible, even for East Anglia.

The mission was to marshaling yards at Untershlauersbach, Nurnberg, Germany, and this meant a long mission. Takeoffs would be with full fuel tanks and full bomb bays.

Flak was expected to be light-to-moderate; they would be escorted by P-51s.

The pre-mission procedures were completed with each crewman having particular assignments such as cleaning the turret windows, warming up engines and radio equipment, and the checking of same, etc.

---

[12] Share had flown his first mission as radioman with Corkern on March 10, 1945.

They had already received their parachutes, put on their heated suits and flight overalls, and over this they donned the pile-lined flight suits and boots, and lastly, their parachute harnesses.

It was near dawn when they were trucked out to "Dinah-Mite"; the weather was still gray with a heavy, wet overcast.

Share had gone to the radiomen's briefing and when he arrived at "Dinah-Mite's" hard stand, the flight engineer, Niatas, had already inspected the aircraft, warmed up the engines, and then shut down the engines so the fuel tanks could be topped up. "Dinah-Mite" would take off with full tanks and full bomb load.

Bob Lampey, ball turret gunner, Lou Morgan, tail gunner, and Al Dienes, waist gunner, had checked their gun stations and were waiting for the officers to arrive from their briefings.

By the time they arrived, Share had checked out the radios.

All boarded "Dinah-Mite" and it was time to watch for a "start engines" green flare; this was seen at 4:45. When the white flare was fired for them to start taxiing, the weather was a steady downpour.

At the sight of the green light from the control building, throttles were pushed forward and the heavy bomber slowly began to roll for its takeoff for deep Germany.

For an hour "Dinah-Mite" climbed to the rallying point over Reims, France. Visibility was zero.

They were instructed to go from 18,000 feet to 25,000 feet altitude. They came out into bright sunlight, located their lead bomber, and maneuvered into their proper position in the formation.

The leader took the formation for another full circuit of the rallying point and turned on the course that would eventually take them to the target. After twenty minutes, the navigator, Britton, informed the crew they were over Germany.

Visibility had gotten worse and the formation climbed to 28,000 feet. The temperature was near -30° F and any moisture turned to frost, then ice. Chemical defrosters weren't removing the ice from turret windows. Because of this, the top turret wasn't usable and a short time later, the ball turret gunner, 18-year-old Lampey, said his turret was also iced over. He was satisfied that he could rotate the turret to the exit position and re-enter the fuselage with the other crewmen.

Britton told the crew they were approaching the I.P. (initial point) to start their bomb run. The P-51s were staying with them though the Luftwaffe was grounded in the thick weather below.

The radar-aimed flak was not "light-to-moderate"; it was very thick with the concussion of some near-misses pounding and flexing "Dinah-Mite's" skin.

Jack Share generally couldn't judge the accuracy of flak from the radio compartment because there were just two small windows, but this time it was heavy and near enough that he could see the flashes of the exploding shells. Share made sure he was wearing his flak jacket and helmet, and that the flak curtain was under his feet.

On these overcast missions when flak was directed by radar, it was the radioman's responsibility to drop chaff down a chute to fall free of the aircraft and confuse the radar operators below.

A flak burst sent shrapnel through the aircraft's nose, barely missing the navigator's head, but it disabled some radio equipment.

The formation had two radar-equipped B-17s and with no visibility of ground features, all bombardiers watched the lead ship and released their bombs when the lead aircraft bombardier released his.

The bomb bay doors were opened and the bombs released.

The radio compartment was separated from the bomb bay by a thin bulkhead and door. At the time of bomb release, Share heard an unusual metal-on-metal banging. He always opened the radio compartment door to make sure everything was clear in the bomb bay. Then he could notify the pilot it was OK to close the bomb bay.

It wasn't OK.

The rear shackle of the lower right bomb was hung up. Share gave it a kick to see if it would clear, but because of their altitude, he could not be off oxygen very long. He went back to his station to notify the pilot of the problem.

The noises had come from some of the other bombs falling onto the bomb now hanging nose down. The bombs most likely exited the aircraft by bouncing off the hung-up bomb and then striking the catwalk in the center of the bomb bay before falling free.

The pilot, Mehling, decided nothing could be done just then about the hung-up bomb and they made their turn and started their descent en route back to England.

Fortunately, the bomb bay doors did close with the nose of the bomb resting against the right door.

At 11,000 feet, bombardier Harris went to the bomb bay, and rendered the bomb relatively safe by replacing the arming pin. Then, as he often did, he sat down in the radio compartment with Share.

Harris was the oldest of the crew, 34 years old, married, and with children. He could have been at home rather than in dangerous skies over Germany, but he wanted to make his contribution as best he could.

The flak-damaged radio equipment prevented the aircraft from transmitting messages, but the aircraft could still receive.

Mehling asked Share to signal the lead ship to their right with the high-wattage Aldis spotlight. This had an on/off trigger permitting the radioman to signal other aircraft by Morse code.

The pilot was permitted to move "Dinah-Mite" from the formation and try to drop the bomb, but they were not to lose sight of the formation...easy to do in the poor visibility.

They were going to be crossing Belgium and then leaving the coast near the Belgium-French border. They hoped to drop the bomb in the North Sea.

They zigzagged around towns and flew so low they could watch scared cattle running across fields.

Britton notified them that the French coast was in sight.

Though Dunkerque had been by-passed by ground forces and was now surrounded, it was still occupied by Germans forces and heavily defended. They knew to pass at least six miles from Dunkerque.

As "Dinah-Mite" approached the coast, Share heard an unfamiliar plinking noise. He thought it could be a partially retracted trailing antenna banging against the aircraft underside. He checked, but that was not the source of noise.

Unfortunately, they were not flying six to eight miles to the southeast of Dunkerque, but directly over it. At their 1,000-foot altitude, almost everything could fire on them. "Dinah-Mite" started receiving hits from 20-mm and 12-mm machine guns.

Share opened the door to the waist gun area and saw the waist gunner, Dienes, standing with a dazed look and blood trickling from under his helmet and down his left cheek.

Share sat back down to hook up his intercom and report to the pilot, but smoke started filling the radio compartment. To breathe, Share put on his oxygen mask.

The flight controls had been shot out and Mehling was flying with throttles only. The #2 engine had stopped and a wing fire had broken out behind that main fuel tank.

The machine guns continued to fire at them.

Share felt terrific pain in both feet as if he had been hit across the feet with a baseball bat.

In all of this, Harris, the bombardier, had remained sitting in the radio compartment.

Shrapnel had rotated Share's swivel chair to face the center of the radio compartment. He looked down to see his right leg swinging wildly like a pendulum and blood gushing out the top of his boot.

Harris stood up and started for him but then grabbed his chest with both hands and crumpled to the floor.

Share's pain was so great he toppled out of his seat.

They were no longer wearing their flak jackets because of their weight, and Share had pushed his flak curtain aside to clear a heater vent near the floor by his seat.

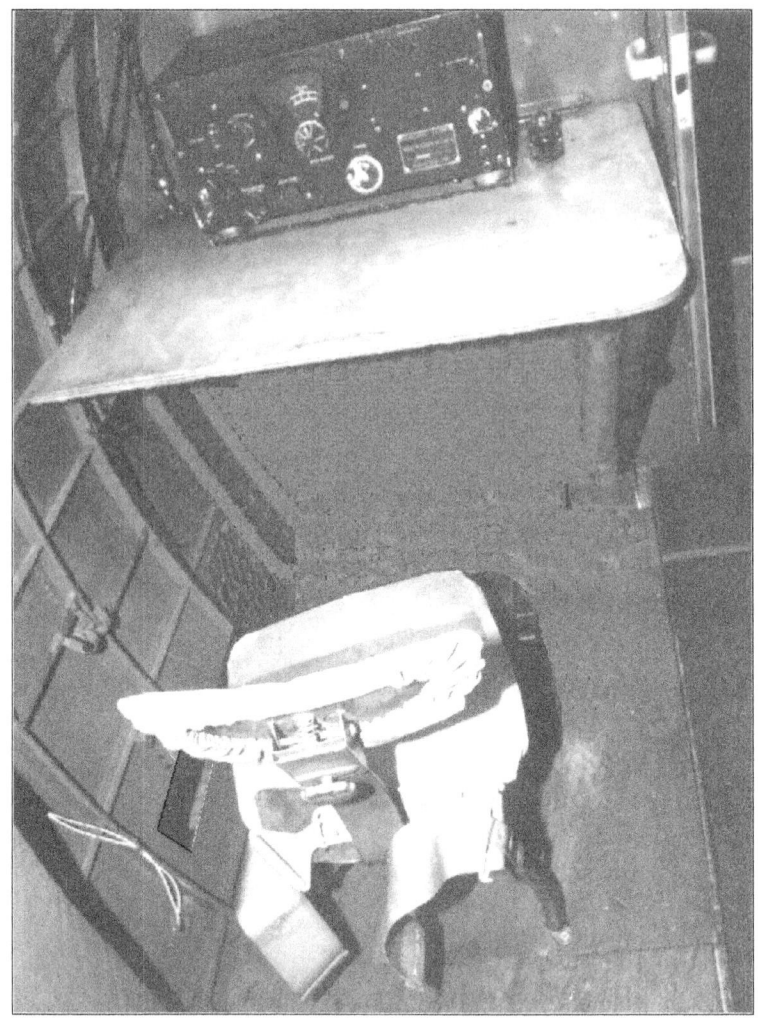

Radioman's station on aircraft left side behind bomb bay.

Upper center is principal 6-band receiver, to right is telegraph key, to far right is edge of open door to bomb bay.

Much equipment is missing in this compartment.

To left of receiver would have been a power inverter. On left wall just above table was where the radioman's oxygen regulator, pressure gauge and flow indicator would have been mounted. A few inches above receiver to the left was the bail-out bell.

Seat style varied but near floor to lower left of seat is the heater duct. *(Cashion photograph)*

Mehling told the crew they were going to ditch in the North Sea, and then Niatas, the flight engineer, came through the bomb bay door into the radio compartment and said the same thing.

Two crewmen picked up Share and put him back in his seat where he should be when ditching. The escape hatch in the top of the radio compartment was released.

Then they started sitting on the right side of the radio compartment floor, one with his back to the forward bulkhead, the next crewman sitting between his legs with his back against the first man's chest, the third crewman between the second's legs with his back to the front of the aircraft. This herringbone position would place a lot of pressure on the first man, but this standard crash position offered the most protection for the crewmen.

Share was yelling, "How am I going to get out of here?" He knew he couldn't stand to reach the overhead escape hatch.

Britton said, "Don't worry, we'll get you out."

Then he asked, "Who is this?" gesturing to Harris. No one answered.

Lou Morgan and Al Dienes were still in the waist gun positions and might not have known they were ditching. The procedure was that the pilot or co-pilot would ring the bell three times, but Share does not recall hearing it and there was a bell within three feet of him. With one engine out, a wing burning, and the pilot was controlling the aircraft attitude using only three throttles – Mehling and co-pilot Huntley might have been too busy to ring a bell, or electric power to the bell might have been interrupted.

They had rehearsed the emergency exit procedure many times and they could clear the aircraft in 12 seconds – in practice.

There was a first hard impact, a smooth skip, and then another hard impact.

The aircraft stopped and cold water started rising in the fuselage.

All this had happened very quickly. They had ditched about a mile from the mouth of the Dunkerque harbor.

The flight engineer operated the release to free the two life rafts from an external storage bay just forward of the emergency hatch.

(Cashion photograph)

This B-17 has early color scheme and markings, as well as an older tail gun configuration. Open hatch above "R" is emergency exit in radio compartment. Forward of exit is compartment ceiling window and to lower right of exit is side window; another window is on left side. On top between exit and top turret were life raft compartments, one on each side.

Share saw crewmen leaving the aircraft through the ceiling hatch and he thinks he saw someone go through an opening in the side of the fuselage. The fuselage had split open at the radio compartment.

Lampey had helped Niatas climb through the escape hatch and followed after him. Not all the crew were wearing Mae West life preservers, and some who were, didn't inflate them.

Lampey jumped into the sea to keep one of the life rafts from floating away.

With the fuselage broken open, the aircraft was sinking fast. No doubt lifting Share's weight through the hatch in a rolling sea, from the top of a wet, sinking aircraft, would have been very difficult.

Share started hobbling on his knees to the split in the fuselage. He was attempting to pull himself out, but the waves were rough, the fuselage edges jagged, and with wave motion, the split was opening and closing. He was having a difficult time getting high enough.

There was a push in his rear, but he doesn't know "who" did this or perhaps, "what" did it. There was a lot of confusion and he was badly wounded. He could have been "pushed on" by the heavy transmitter that had come loose, but he became free of the aircraft at the wing.

Share rolled off the wing into the water and saw that Niatas was on the wing and Lampey was exhausted from trying to tow the raft back. He could get no closer than 25 feet – Share started dog-paddling to the raft.

By the time Share got to the raft, Lampey had gotten in and Niatas was hanging on the side. Share couldn't pull himself in. All this was done with the crewmen still in their heavy flight suits, but they were buoyant until they became saturated with water.

Niatas got in the raft and he and Lampey pulled Share in. Share said later that when he was pulled in, he had felt no pain but noticed he had lost his right boot.

Lampey and Niatas used the paddles to get to the tail section and meet the raft that had been released from the other side of the aircraft.

It was occupied by the pilot, Mehling; tail gunner, Lou Morgan; and Britton, navigator.

Dienes was standing on the wing and after hesitating a second, jumped into the sea and floated with his inflated Mae West toward the tail. When he reached the tail, he took hold of the stabilizer.

He was yelling that he couldn't swim – though he had just floated from the wing to the tail. Then the aircraft started to settle and those in the rafts were yelling for him to let go and they would paddle over and get him.

He refused, or was unable to force himself to release his grip.

Then the nose slid under the water and "Dinah-Mite" went down with Dienes still holding to the tail. Also going down was Harris, dead in the radio compartment.

Co-pilot Huntley had also not exited the aircraft. He was a large man and the flight compartment escape windows were small; he could have become hung up at the co-pilot window opening. The pilot said that he, himself, had been snagged for a moment while exiting through his window on the left side.

It was said that "Dinah-Mite" stayed afloat, even with the tear in her side, for a minute to a minute and a half.

The two rafts were tied together and the men started bailing.

As they were bobbing in the rafts, Share's limp right foot would sometimes fall over the edge of the raft. Mehling placed Share's feet together, took off his own flight jacket and wrapped it around Share's feet to hold them in place. Mehling would suffer from the cold even more because of his kind act. At least the cold salt water had slowed Share's bleeding.

They were cheered when a B-17 circled over them a few times. They said that surely he was sending their position to rescue crews.

A half-hour later, they heard a single-engine aircraft approaching. Seeing that it was friendly, Mehling started shooting flares. The P-47 was from an RAF Air Sea Rescue unit. It circled low and dropped dye markers and a smoke canister.

After another fifteen minutes, two more P-47s arrived, and then three Spitfires came over them. This was not only comforting but they could be a source of protection if needed.

—o–o–O–o–o—

Then a very strange thing happened which points out that it was, at all times, dangerous everywhere in this theater of war. One of the three Spitfires developed engine trouble and started losing altitude. The pilot was trying to get the engine cleared and avoid losing more altitude.

When down to about 100 feet above the water, he apparently stalled the Spitfire. It snap-rolled, crashing into the sea inverted.

The crew tried to paddle to where it had crashed but no pilot was found.

As the Spitfire pilot had approached the two rafts, he might have thought, 'Those poor guys. They've had some tough luck today,' and he might have been thinking about how fortunate he had been and what he would be enjoying while those unfortunate crewmen suffered wet and cold.

Then his engine misfired...

—o–o–O–o–o—

After another hour of the crew bailing water and shaking from the cold, a Catalina flying boat came over. Because of the waves, it couldn't land but the Catalina crew did drop a message on a little parachute. Like a lot of things falling into the sea, it disappeared before it could be recovered.

They were constantly soaked and the cold would become more intense in the following five hours. It was getting dark and they were now starting to worry.

Share does not remember much happening because early on Lampey had retrieved the first aid kit and given him a shot of morphine. Share recalls a P-47 flying over and hearing something about a Spitfire crashing.

He does remember, however, that Niatas gave him a stick of gum and it tasted good.[13]

Share was moderately comfortable for the five hours, but as the morphine was wearing off, he could see it was getting dark. Then he looked to his right and announced that he could see an antenna. It was not a morphine-induced apparition; a boat was approaching.

—o-o-O-o-o—

In the late afternoon of that April 5th, Aubrey Meadowcroft was on standby at Ostend, Belgium. He was Coxswain (skipper) of 2579 HSL (High Speed Launch) of the RAF Mobile Air Sea Rescue Unit. Ostend is approximately 30 miles north of Dunkerque. Then he received a call that an American plane had crashed off Dunkerque. While speeding the HSL to the area, a P-47 came over to guide him to the two rafts.

The water was rough and they were concerned about the mines blocking the entrance to the Dunkerque harbor. The skipper did not have those charts.

---

[13] Other survivors remember seeing poor Share, badly shot up, in a desperate situation, leaning back in a morphine bliss, nonchalantly chewing gum, and this cheered them.

The boat crew located the rafts and eased up to them. The "Dinah-Mite" crewmen were too tired and cold to pull themselves from the rafts. They were lifted onboard and the boat's crew sank the rafts with machine gun fire. The rafts had been the crew's last contact with "Dinah-Mite."

The boat hurriedly departed because Germans started firing at them with an 88-mm cannon.

"Dinah-Mite's" crew were literally carried to the warm crew compartment, given hot soup, and a large shot of rum. They received dry clothes and a bunk. The boat's doctor said that Share was in good condition – considering.

It was getting dark and it would be more than a two-hour trip back to Ostend. Since they had a badly wounded crewman onboard, the throttles of the HSL were set to maximum.

There was a "gate" on the throttles which allowed the boat its highest speed – but for only fifteen minutes. The throttles were kept past this gate for at least two hours.

When the crewmen were put ashore at Ostend, the center engine was glowing red. It had gotten them back to their berth but the center engine was removed and it never ran again.

The motto of the RAF Air Sea Rescue Service was "The Sea Shall Not Have Them."

Share was sped by ambulance to the 105th British Hospital in Ostend. The rest of the crew went to a small field hospital.

In the British Hospital, Share had surgery to remove the lower part of his right leg and repair the damage done to his left. He received excellent care.

The second day in the hospital, his fellow crewmates visited him. They were happy to be alive but still grieved their three dead friends.

Because there had been a failure of communication between the RAF rescue services and the 8th AAF, the crewmen were listed as MIA. They were unexpected arrivals back at Mendlesham!

After physical exams at the Mendlesham base hospital, they were sent to Bournemouth, England, for a two-week rest.

The day after the crew had seen Share, Aubrey Meadowcroft, the Coxswain of the rescue launch, visited.

The two RAF pilots who had circled the rafts also visited him. They, too, were grieving a missing flight mate.

Share was transported to an American hospital in England and then flown to a US hospital.

—o–o–O–o–o—

Share's pilot, George Mehling, flew one more mission after the loss of "Dinah-Mite" and three crewmates. On May 7, he flew a mercy mission, Mx. #176, to drop food to the Dutch. And he was flying 960 B/L. (The Corkern, Reid, and Kennedy B-17.)

Jack Share had flown his first mission in B-17G – 960 B/L and now his pilot had made his last mission in the same aircraft.

—o–o–O–o–o—

In June, 1945, Niatas flew back to the US as flight engineer on B-17G "Little Gizmo." He received his discharge that year at Roswell, New Mexico.

—o–o–O–o–o—

It was a little over two months from the time Jack Share had been wounded until he could put weight on his left foot. His rehabilitation continued until eventually he was fitted with a prosthesis. He would need to demonstrate that he could walk with just a cane and pass a driver's test before he could be discharged from the military.

On May 19, 1946, Jack Share received his discharge and returned to civilian life.

—o–o–O–o–o—

In 1995, Jack Share and George Mehling met with Aubrey Meadowcroft again. Meadowcroft is the only former RAF member with membership in the 34th Bomb Group Association.

Jack Share was the Editor of the 34th Bomb Group Association newsletter, *Mendlesham Memories.*

—o–o–O–o–o—

The author spoke at length with Share, who provided much of the information presented here. Other information came from the writings of Stephen Niatas, and the writings of Aubrey Meadowcroft.

—o–o–O–o–o—

Appendix - F

NAMES OF AIRCRAFT IN WHICH CORKERN FLEW

Name	Military #	Radio #	Mx.	Returned to US
"Maid of (Fury?)"	43-38338	B/M	49	No - Lost in mid-air collision.
"Hit & Run"	43-38391	E/J	50	Yes w/34th BGp
"Bottoms Up"	43-38326	B/U	53	Yes - There was another "Bottoms Up" in the 34th BGp, 48309 E/H, but it did not return.
"Flying Dutchmen"	43-38286	E/T	83	Yes
"Marge"	44-6840	B/E	39	Yes
"Betty"	43-38409	B/B	71	Yes
"Ol' Buddy"	44-8309	E/H	36	Yes
"Tempest Turner"	43-38216	B/O	29	Yes w/34th BGp.
"Goin' My Way!"	43-37960	B/L	36	Yes - But crewmembers did not know it by this name. No nose art.

"Evadin' Maiden" 44-6929 B/Q 40   Yes - Flown to US by A.
Pierre. He had flown Mx.
168 in 960 B/L.

"Little Gizmo" 44-6938 B/G 39   Yes - Flown to US by J.
Novicki. He had flown Mx.
161 in 960 B/L

B-17G-60-VE   44-8321   B/F.
Flown by Kennedy crew on Mx. #114; their second mission attempt and 321 B/F's 28th of more than 70. Aircraft was returned to the US at war's end. *(Gary Ferrell photograph source)*

"Betty"; 43-38409 B/B. The Kennedy crew flew 3 of aircraft's 71 missions.

(Corkern photograph source)

"Flying Dutchmen" 43-38286 E/T. Kennedy crew flew 3 of aircraft's 83 missions. *(Paul Gustafson photograph source)*

"Ol' Buddy" 44-8309 E/H. Kennedy crew flew 1 of aircraft's 36 missions.
(USAF photograph)

Appendix - G

FLIGHT HISTORY OF B-17G-75-BO, 43-37960

WITH JAMES U. CORKERN MISSION LOG

The bulk of this material is from 8th AAF and 34th BGp records and James U. Corkern material. Other sources are listed.

Details from Corkern's mission log are shown in italics as they were entered with only slight modification of spelling and punctuation for accuracy. The author's comments are in brackets.

—o–o–O–o–o—

B-17G-75-BO 43-37960 "Going My Way!"

[Roy Reid, navigator on 960 B/L for many missions, told the author he did not remember it having a name and there was no nose art when they were flying it.]

Aircraft History

June 9, 1944 sent from Boeing factory to Cheyenne, Wyoming, for modifications.

June 21, 1944 to Kearney Airfield, Nebraska.

July 9, 1944 to Grenier Field, Manchester, New Hampshire.

July 12, 1944 Assigned to 34th Bomb Group, Mendlesham, East Anglia, England.

The 34th BGp was still operating B-24s at this date. They transitioned to B-17s about September 1, 1944. The first B-17 mission for 34th BGp was September 17, 1944.

Mission (Mx. #) **Date** **Aircraft**
BSq **Pilot**
  Target

Mission #112 January 14, 1945 43-38338 – B/M
18BSq Kennedy

Target was oil storage depot at Derben. We were briefed for no flak but ran into secret gun installations and lost two planes out of our lead squadron. No one got out. Dropped bombs and fighters hit division. The G.A.F. [German Air Force] *lost 180 fighters. The most on one raid since war started. Gunners got 31 and our P-51 escort got 149. We got one hole by flak and returned safely.* [Germany – oil storage facility was underground]

Mission #114 January 16, 1945 44-8321 – B/F
18BSq Kennedy

[The next attempted mission was not credited but is presented here for accuracy.]

Was an abort. We were in formation and No. 3 turbo ran away and we had to turn back. The lead plane we were flying formation with caught fire at #3 engine. All of the crew bailed out but ball gunner was killed by falling in the wreckage of the burning plane. Our field was closed in and we landed at a Limey base.

[BGp records indicate that the explosion from the crashing bomber collapsed the gunner's parachute and he was killed by the fall.]

Mission (Mx. #) **Date** **Aircraft**

BSq **Pilot**

Target

Mission #115 January 20, 1945 43-38286 – E/T

18BSq Kennedy

Target was oil laboratories at Hamburg in the Rhur valley, better known to us as "Happy Valley." We were briefed for 300 guns around the target. We lost #1 engine first over the target but got it going again just as we lost #4. We managed to drop bombs on the target. No enemy fighters were reported. We had to fall out of formation over the target and make it back to England alone except for an escort of P-51s. They sure looked good to us because stragglers don't last long over Germany. We got four flak holes today. Pieces of flak hit Roy in the head but his flak helmet saved him from injury. Mission was completed safely.

Mission #116 January 23, 1945 43-38391– E/J

18BSq Kennedy

Target was rail yards at Neuss. We didn't have a bit of trouble this trip. No Jerry fighters were reported but flak was quite heavy and pretty accurate for barrage. Seven ships lost engines due to flak. The mission was completed safely. On mission 2 [Mx. #115 - Jan. 20], I got a little frost bite on my right ear but it was fine today.

Mission (Mx. #)	Date	Aircraft
BSq	**Pilot**	
	Target	

Mission #121 February 9, 1945   43-38326 – B/U
18BSq   Kennedy

Target today was Wensl in "Happy Valley." It was a bridge the army had requested destroyed. We again had to drop out of formation. We dropped our bombs and started out alone. We were forced down in Brussels in Belgium. Had a wonderful time but left almost immediately. I guess Lady Luck must be riding with us. Again no fighters attacked.

Mission #122 February 14, 1945   43-38338 – B/M
18BSq   Kennedy

Target was a marshaling yard at a small town just south of Berlin. Mostly to help Russians. We did a fine job on the target. No fighters hit us but I saw a couple of dog fights by our escort. We didn't lose any of our engines today. It was mostly a milk run but we came out through "Happy Valley." I guess we will go out again tomorrow if weather holds out.

[Target was listed in BGp records as Chemnitz]

Mission #123 February 15, 1945   44-6840 – B/E
18BSq   Kennedy

Target was marshaling yards at Cottbus. No flak was seen. The mission was 9 hrs. and 10 mins. long.

Mission (Mx. #)	Date	Aircraft
BSq	**Pilot**	
	Target	

Mission #124 February 17, 1945   44-6840 – B/E
18BSq   Kennedy

Target was center of town at Frankfurt. Our bombs had to be dropped by hand. We missed the main target but hit two small towns. Again we had no flak.

Mission #126 February 20, 1945   44-6840 – B/E
18BSq   Kennedy

Target was marshaling yards at Nurnberg. Plenty of flak but it wasn't accurate today. We had four good engines and didn't get a single hole. There were around 150 guns on the target areas. It was a long haul.

Mission #127 February 21, 1945   43-38409– B/B
18BSq   Kennedy

Target was marshaling yards at Nurnberg. There was plenty of flak and it was accurate. We got at least ten holes but everyone returned safe. A piece hit my B.T. glass [ball turret sighting window] *and broke it. Good thing it is bullet proof. Had four good engines.*

Mission #133 March 1, 1945   44-8309 – E/H
18BSq   Kennedy

Target was marshaling yards at Olm. It was a long haul but not much flak. The crew is still together.

Mission (Mx. #)	Date	Aircraft
BSq	**Pilot**	
	Target	

Mission #134 March 2, 1945   43-38216 –B/O

18BSq   Kennedy

Target was center of town at Dresden. There was no flak at the target but fighters hit us from I.P. to R.P. Mickey, Thomas, and Roy got credit for a Jerry fighter. One squadron lost three planes. One gunner killed in our outfit. Planes all blew up. P-51 got 66 Jerries in the air and 38 on the ground! I was scared. The crew is still together.

[I.P. is Initial Point which begins the flight line to the bomb release. R.P. is the Rally Point where formations regroup and turn for exit from target area.]

Mission #135 March 3, 1945   43-38409 – B/B

18BSq   Kennedy

Target was center of town at Bielefeld. No flak was close but we saw a damn good dog fight behind us. No fighters attacked us today. Hope the luck holds out. The crew is still together. I am pretty tired. Probably fly tomorrow.

Mission #136 March 4, 1945   43-38409 – B/B

18BSq   Kennedy

Target was ammo dump at Dortmouth. This was a good mission. Not too much flak but it was in "Happy Valley."

[The mission was recalled. Bombs dropped in safe zone.]

Mission (Mx. #)　　**Date**　　　　　　**Aircraft**
　　BSq　　　**Pilot**
　　　　　　　Target

Mission #137　March 7, 1945　　　43-37960 – B/L
18BSq　　　　Kennedy

I forgot what the target was but we didn't get to go there because clouds were too high. We went over the battle lines and got flak and had to return on account of weather. We brought our bombs back but got credit for a mission. Two planes were lost due to weather and collision. One of our good buddies was in the crash. I sure did hate it.

[BGp records show mid-air to have occurred on Mx. #136. This mission was to Datteln, target was to be synthetic fuel plant.]

Mission #138　March 8, 1945　　　43-37960 – B/L
18BSq　　　　Hemingway

[Kennedy crew stood down and Hemingway, another 18th BSq pilot, flew aircraft on mission to Dortmund.]

Mission #139　March 10, 1945　　　43-37960 – B/L
18BSq　　　　Kennedy

Target was marshaling yards at Soest. It is also in "Happy Valley" but the flak wasn't accurate. We didn't get any fighters or flak holes. We carried leaflets and money and ration points but the rest of the Group carried 42-100 pounders. We have been assigned a new ship. No. 960 L - for love.

[Crew had already flown mission in 960 B/L on Mar. 7.]

Mission (Mx. #)	Date	Aircraft
BSq	**Pilot**	
	Target	

Mission #142 March 14, 1945   43-37960 – B/L
[Aircraft was used as mission backup.]

Mission #143 March 15, 1945   43-37960 – B/L
18BSq   Kennedy
Target was marshaling yards just on the outskirts of Berlin. We got flak from Berlin and just about every other place. We ran into some secret flak guns but didn't lose any planes. I sure do like our new plane. The crew is still together. We didn't get any fighters today.
[Target was Orenienburg.]

Mission #144 March 17, 1945   43-37960 – B/L
18BSq   Kennedy
Target was Bitterfeld. There was no flak on the target but we got some after leaving the target. All close calls. I had my oxygen line cut and some wires. Cleo [Baughman] *had a close one, too, and Mick's was real close. Everyone returned safe.*

Mission #145 March 18, 1945   43-37960 – B/L
18BSq   Kennedy
Target was Berlin and we really tore the hell out of it. Flak was pretty heavy but we only got one hole. Almost had to land in Russia.

Mission (Mx. #)	Date	Aircraft
BSq	Pilot	
	Target	

Mission #146 March 19, 1945   43-37960 – B/L
18BSq   Kennedy

Target was Jena. The flak wasn't too heavy and no fighter attacks. We got one hole. One ship had #1 engine blown off but got back. The crew is still together.

Mission #148 March 21, 1945   43-37960 – B/L
18BSq   Kennedy

Target today was an air field at Marx. The flak wasn't bad and no fighters hit.

Mission #149 March 22, 1945   43-37960 – B/L
18BSq   Kennedy

Target today were German troops at Regan. We got excellent results. The flak wasn't too bad but there was plenty. The crew is still together with the exception of Mick.

[BGp records has target as German headquarters at Ratingen.]

Mission #150 March 23, 1945   43-37960 – B/L
18BSq   Kennedy

Target today was a marshaling yard in the Dartmuth area. This was a pretty rough mission. Not much flak but it was accurate. We lost two planes. This looks like the beginning of something big.

[BGp records has Geisecke marshaling yards as target.]

Mission (Mx. #)	Date	Aircraft
BSq	Pilot	
	Target	

Mission #151 March 24, 1945   43-37960 – B/L
391BSq   Sykes

[Target was Zwischenahn. Sykes, a pilot from 391st BSq flew aircraft. Kennedy crew had a six-day rest with exception of Roy Reid who flew with Sykes this day.]

Mission #152 March 26, 1945   43-37960 – B/L
18BSq   Mann

[Target was Planen. Mann, another 18th BSq pilot and crew flew aircraft.]

Mission #153 March 28, 1945   43-37960 – B/L
18BSq   Novicki

[Target was Hannover & Mindemn. Novicki, another 18th BSq pilot and crew flew aircraft.]

Mission #154 March 30, 1945   43-37960 – B/L
18BSq   Kennedy

Target today was submarine pens at Hamburg. There were 280 guns at the target. Fighters hit us today. They were 262 jet jobs and they shot almost all of our tail off. Rough mission. The crew is still together. 300 holes. You can't beat a 17 for coming back shot up.

[Corkern lists this mission as occurring on 3-29-45. BGp records shows no mission that day.]

Mission (Mx. #)   **Date**   **Aircraft**

BSq   **Pilot**

          Target

Mission #155 March 31, 1945   44-6929 – H/E

18BSq   Kennedy

Target today was Brandenburg. The flak wasn't too bad. The clouds and haze was rough. No Jerry fighters came up. Hope they stay down. I have seen enough of them. The crew is still together.   [Target was armored car factory.]

Mission #156 April 3, 1945   43-37960 – B/L

18BSq   Kennedy

Target today was sub pens and the rest of the German navy at Kiel. The flak wasn't too bad but you could see the fire when it exploded. No fighters opposed us. I sure hope they stay down after last trip.

      [Meaning "last trip" in 960 B/L.]

Mission #157 April 4, 1945   43-37960 – B/L

18BSq   Kennedy

Target today was Kiel. The flak was pretty heavy and was some of the biggest they had ever shot at us. We were lucky and didn't get any holes. No fighters hit us but they were up.

      [Returned to bomb fleet.]

Mission (Mx. #)   **Date**   **Aircraft**
BSq   **Pilot**
            Target

Mission #158   April 5, 1945   43-37960 – B/L
18BSq   Kennedy

Target today was Nurnburg. This sure is a rough target. Today was our third trip there and there is plenty of flak but it wasn't accurate today. No fighters were up. Hope they never get up.

Mission #159   April 7, 1945   43-37960 – B/L
18BSq   Kennedy

Target today was Gustrow just north of Berlin. Jerry fighters hit us from the battle line to the I.P., a total of 50 minutes. The crew is still together. I hit a Me-109 but didn't knock him down, a P-51 got him. Planes were blowing up all around. I was just waiting our time but it never came. There were about 150 enemy fighters. Lord ride with us if it is thy will. We destroyed 104.

[Target was important ordnance depot supplying Eastern Front.]

Mission #160   April 8, 1945   43-37960 – B/L
18BSq   Kennedy

Target today was Grafenwhor. Jerry was up again today, but didn't hit us. The flak wasn't bad but we went in at 14,000 ft. We were fighter bait today and destroyed around 80. Hope the luck holds out.

[Target was ordnance depot and Wehrmacht barracks.]

Mission (Mx. #)	Date	Aircraft
BSq	Pilot	
	Target	

Mission #161 April 9, 1945   43-37960 – B/L
18BSq   Novicki
[Kennedy's crew stood down. Novicki, another 18th BSq pilot flew aircraft. Target was Schlissheim.]

Mission #163 April 11, 1945   43-37960 – B/L
18BSq   Kennedy
Target today was a marshaling yard in a small town close to Nurnburg. No flak or fighters today. It was a good mission.
[BGp records have Treuchtlengen as target.]

Mission #164 April 14, 1945   44-6938 – B/C
18BSq   Kennedy
Target today was Royan in France on the coast. This was a milk run.
[Mission was scheduled for 43-37960 but aircrew was switched to 44-6938.]

Mission #165 April 15, 1945   43-37960 – B/L
18BSq   Kennedy
Target today was Royan in France. It was a milk run again. The French took it right after we bombed. The coast is really tore up.

Mission (Mx. #)	Date	Aircraft
BSq	**Pilot**	
	Target	

Mission #166   April 16, 1945   43-37960 – B/L
18BSq   Kennedy
Target today was Granepoint, France. It was a milk run. No fighters. No nothing. I sure was glad too. This does it for us. <u>The End.</u>

[Double underlines are in Corkern's mission log. This was Corkern's last mission. Target was German coastal guns in Royan area. They had been bypassed by ground forces.]

Mission #167   April 17, 1945   43-37960 – B/L
          [Aircraft was used for mission backup.]

Mission #168   April 18, 1945   43-37960 – B/L
18BSq   Pierre
          [Targets were Kolin & Passau.]

Mission #169   April 19, 1945   43-37960 – B/L
18BSq   Edwards
          [Target was Aussig.]

Mission #170   April 20, 1945   43-37960 – B/L
18BSq   Agegian
          [Target was Nauen. This was seventh mission in seven days for 960 B/L.]

Mission (Mx. #)	Date	Aircraft
BSq	Pilot	
	Target	

Mission #171　May 1, 1945　　　43-37960 – B/L
391BSq　　　Gulmetti
[Scheduled, then scratched, but then apparently flew anyway.]

Mission #172　May 2, 1945　　　43-37960 – B/L
18BSq　　　Tennent
[Operation Chowhound food drop in Holland.]

Mission #173　May 3, 1945　　　43-37960 – B/L
18BSq　　　Buchanan
[Operation Chowhound food drop.]

Mission #174　May 5, 1945　　　43-37960 – B/L
18BSq　　　Buchanan
[Operation Chowhound food drop.]

Mission #175　May 6, 1945　　　43-37960 – B/L
18BSq　　　Tennent
[Operation Chowhound food drop.]

Mission #176　May 7, 1945　　　43-37960 – B/L
18BSq　　　Mehling
[Operation Chowhound food drop. Mehling had been the pilot of "Dinah-Mite" and Jack Share when it went down off Dunkerque.]

Mission (Mx. #)	Date	Aircraft
BSq	**Pilot**	
	Target	

Mission #177 May 15, 1945　　43-37960 – B/L
18BSq　　Stewart
(POW and displaced person transport.)

—o-o-O-o-o—

June 21, 1945　　43-37960
Chapman
Returned to US, Bradley Field, Connecticut
(Chapman had crews #48 and #34 onboard.)

June 22, 1945　　43-37960
Flown to 4168 BU (converging depot) South Plains
Fields, Lubbock, Texas

December 19, 1945　43-37960
Flown to Kingman, Arizona. Last flight.

—o-o-O-o-o—

Appendix - H

OPERATION CHOWHOUND

In September 1944, the Allied ground forces had begun "Operation Market-Garden." This was a major advance through the low countries.

The Dutch had been asked to call a labor strike on the Dutch Railway to make it difficult for many of the German occupation forces in Holland to reach the combat area.

In retaliation, the Germans forbade farm produce from the country being delivered to the cities by rail. As city food supplies were being reduced to a dangerously low level, Western Europe experienced an unusually harsh winter.

The people in the Dutch cities were starving to death. The Dutch Queen-in-Exile requested emergency support from the allies so an assistance program was developed and Germany agreed to a local truce.

The plan involved major food drops at nine Dutch sites. These would be over crater-strewn runways of airports, city fairgrounds, racing circuits – anywhere there was a sufficiently clear area.

If an aircraft's route was over a designated corridor, it would not be fired on. If, however, it strayed from that route, warning flak would be fired. These would have red bursts but no shrapnel.

Apparently, this agreement was forgotten and real flak was fired. There are no records of aircraft damage from this flak, however.

The RAF started dropping food on April 29, 1945. Their phase of the operation was known as Manna. The 8th AAF, including 18th BSq, started Operation Chowhound on May 1.

The combined food drops totaled 10,827 tons delivered by 5,024 flights.

When the hungry citizens heard the approach of the bombers, people of all ages ran into the streets waving flags and scarves. From the drop altitude of 500 feet, crewmen could see dancing in the streets.

The 34th BGp primarily dropped "Ten-in-One" rations: canned meat, butter, bread, jam, etc. Sacks of flour were dropped, as well.

The B-17 had not been designed to drop food, so the bomb bays had to be modified with plywood floors attached to bomb shackles. The food was loaded on the plywood, the aircraft approached the drop site, the bomb bay doors were opened, and one edge of the plywood was released, dropping the food.

It was reported that 1,000 Dutch had been starving each day.

Manna from Heaven, indeed.

Both operations stopped on May 8 – VE-Day.

—o–o–O–o–o—

Appendix - I

CREW AND PASSENGER LIST FOR

B-17G-75-BO, s/n 43-37960 (960B/L)

RETURN TO AMERICA

Crewman	Military I.D. Assignment Code
Pilot – 1Lt. Karl Chapman, Jr.	O-836580 1091
Co-Pilot – 2Lt. William C. Drennan	O-930383 1091
Navigator – 2Lt. Dale Livingston	O-2075242 1034
Bombardier – 1Lt. James L. Ford	O-739460 1035
Radio Operator – T/Sgt. Garth D. Dawson	36680818 757
Flight Engineer – T/Sqt. Vernon L. Evans	17047203 748

Crewman	Military I.D. Assignment Code
Gunner – S/Sgt. Cherry Harrgunn	36863398 611
Gunner – S/Sgt. Raymond A. Safer	38239692 612
Gunner – Marvin O. Wilkerson	34924081 612
Crew Chief – S/Sgt. Mitchell C. Turek	11071147 750
Passenger – Capt. James A. Stewart	O-1166387 1091
Passenger – 1Lt. Lawrence D. Underwood	O-698056 1035
Passenger – Cpl. Ward A. Yarbrough	38583164 612
Passenger – Sgt. Jacob Stockman	34385781 747
Passenger – Sgt. George W. Lentner	37271541 060

Crewman	Military I.D. Assignment Code
Passenger – Sgt. Rynear H. Yale	32385389 060
Passenger – Cpl. Clarence C. Hawkins	38430413 590
Passenger – Cpl. Joseph E. Breslin	39102423 405
Passenger – Sgt. Richard E. Blake	31184126 747
Passenger – Cpl. Billy E. Squire	39283603 911

—o–o–O–o–o—

Appendix - J

THE SCRAP YARDS

The political thinking immediately after WWII was, in one sense, dwelling on the difficulties of dealing with the concessions given to the Soviet Union and the yet-to-be-defined Cold War, but there were still the immediate concerns with the national postwar economy.

The economy would be shifting from a wartime labor force consisting of many women, to trying to accommodate the returning servicemen. These veterans were expecting to enjoy the things for which they had been fighting.

Besides the many social changes of independent women now becoming housewives and mothers, there was the phenomenon known as Levittown, the beginning of suburbia and mass-produced houses in subdivisions.

Additionally, there would be the expense of maintaining some of the many military bases and the disposition of a tremendous amount of military equipment and materiel.

Much of this equipment was left or scrapped in the theatre of war where it was last used, but still a lot of it was returned home. A small amount would be refurbished for future use; the majority would be scrapped.

Typical of many of the aircraft scrap yards was Altus, Oklahoma.[14]

---

[14] Much of this appendix is from "The Daily Oklahoman," Sunday, Feb. 10, 1945, edition. The planes were still arriving as Mark Sarchet, the journalist, was preparing his article.

Altus had a mile and a half square parking lot of aircraft and major aircraft parts. Parts such as props were resting entwined in four-abreast lines a quarter of a mile long.

There were 3,670 radial engines, complete with cowlings, all aligned in rows. They had been removed just after their aircraft had landed and taxied to its last parking place. The engines were perfectly serviceable.

There were over 2,621 aircraft in neat rows. This equipment had been worth near1/2 billion 1940 tax payers' dollars.

Everything on the field was for sale, but most would become scrap.

A private company had been contracted to dispose of it and the first thing sold was the aircraft fuel, almost as soon as the aircraft was taxied into place.

The previous winter, over 3,000 gallons of antifreeze had been sold from the liquid-cooled fighter engines.

Airworthy P-38 Lightnings were priced at $1,250[15]; few to none would be sold. P-61 Black Widows were $6,000 but this price would be out-of-reach because of the limited commercial application for such an aircraft. There were other fighter choices; P-40, P-47, P-51.

An up-to-date bomber such as a B-29 was $32,000. An earlier bomber such as a B-17, B-24, or B-25 was much less.

And there were transports...one with ten camels painted on the side...one for each trip over the "Hump" carrying supplies across the Himalayas.

The better prices were for new aircraft; 300 different types had come straight from the factory to the scrap yard. Ground crews would

---

[15] Equivalent to $12,500 in 2005 dollars. This is near 1:10 due to inflation.

run the engines a few minutes each day in hope that someone would buy one and promptly fly it out.

There were famous aircraft like "Pistol Packin' Mama." It had made over a hundred missions into Europe. (There had been another B-17 with a similar name, "Betty Boop Pistol Packin' Mama," but it was shot down in Europe.)

"Lonesome Baby" made 125 missions over Europe.

There was the B-24, "Five Grand." This was the 5,000th B-24 built and it still had the names of the 200,000 individuals who bought war bonds to earn the privilege of having their name in the wartime skies of WWII.

Another famous aircraft was sitting at Altus awaiting either a buyer or a cutting torch. This was B-17F-10-BO s/n 41-24485 and it had a price tag of just $13,750. It was one of the very few that did survive the scrap yard. It is now on display in Memphis, Tennessee: the familiar "Memphis Belle."

—o–o–O–o–o—

But B-17G-80-BO, s/n 43-37960, aka "960 B/L" did not survive the scrap yard in Kingman, Arizona.

"960 B/L" just wasn't famous enough.

—o–o–O–o–o—

Appendix - K

REFERENCES

1 – USAAF AIRFIELDS, Return To England
-1942-1992; East Anglia Tourist Board.

2 – AMERICAN WARPLANES OF WORLD WAR II;
Barnes & Noble, Inc.

3 – HITLER'S LUFTWAFFE; Tony Wood & Bill
Gunston; Crescent Books

4 – WARPLANES & AIR BATTLES OF WORLD
WAR II; Beekman House.

5 – RAND McNALLY ENCYCLOPEDIA OF
MILITARY AIRCRAFT – 1914 to 1980; Crescent
Books.

6 – THE HISTORY OF THE ARMY AIR FORCE'S 34TH
BOMBARDMENT GROUP (H), 1941 - 1945;
reprint of 1947 edition; The Battery Press, Inc.

7 – 34TH BOMBARDMENT GROUP HISTORY; 1999
edition

8 – MENDLESHAM MEMORIES; Newsletter of the 34th
Bomb Group Association; 34th Bomb Group
Association

9 – B-17 IN ACTION; Series #63; Squadron/Signal
Publications

10 – WALK AROUND – B-17 FLYING FORTRESS; Series
#16; Squadron/Signal Publications

11 – B-17 FLYING FORTRESS UNITS; Osprey Books

12 – THE LUFTWAFFE WAR DIARIES; Cajus Bekker;
Ballentine Books

13 – JANE'S YEARBOOKS; Doubleday Press

14 – AIR FACTS AND FEATS; Doubleday & Company

15 – THE AMERICAN AIRMAN IN EUROPE; Rodger
        A. Freeman; Motorbooks International

16 – AIR FORCE; Martin Cadin; Bramhall Books

17 – THE DOMESDAY BOOK; Crown Publishers

18 – "Dinghy, Dinghy, Dinghy" – Stephan Niatas; Flight
        Engineer, B-17 Dinah-Mite, 34th BGp

19 – Personal writings of James U. Corkern, Sr., ball turret
        gunner, 34th BGp

20 – Personal writings of William F. Cheek, gunner, 34th BGp

21 – Personal writings of and conversations with Jack K.
        Share, radioman, 34th BGp

22 – Personal writings of and conversations with Roy L. Reid,
        navigator, 34th BGp

23 – Verbal and written correspondence with Donald
        Forsman, ball turret gunner, 34th BGp

24 – Conversation with Merlin Bruning, ball turret gunner,
        34th BGp

25 – Conversation with William Maloney, ball turret gunner,
        454th BGp

26 – Conversation with Claude Conklin, ball turret gunner,
        34th BGp

About the Author

Ken Cashion has written myriad scientific papers and technical procedures during his 37-year engineering career, the last 27 of which were with NASA. He has had nonfiction articles in the national press and, as a historian and Anglophile, he has traveled extensively in Britain and has written and taught three college courses on the social history of Britain from 500,000 BC through 1707 AD.

He continues his writing and research in a small, quiet South Mississippi town.

Printed in Great Britain
by Amazon

45105449R00106